GW00976141

Camper Van Life

By Daniel & Rebekah Lopez-Ferreiro

Camper Van Life by Daniel and Rebekah Lopez-Ferreiro

Copy Editor: Kate Taylor
Design: Katie Elliott
Cover artwork: "Summer Sun" by Rebekah Lopez-Ferreiro © 2016

Copyright © Daniel & Rebekah Lopez-Ferreiro, 2018

First Edition: June 2018

ISBN: 978-1-9996272-0-1

Published by SCV Publishing
(a division of Sussex Campervans Ltd)
Graylands Gateway - Langhurst Wood Road
Horsham - West Sussex - RH12 4QD
(Co. Reg no. 8086997)

All Rights Reserved - Worldwide. No part of this publication may be
reproduced, stored in a retrieval system, or transmitted in any
form or by any means - electronic, photocopying, recording or
otherwise - unless the written permission of the publisher has been
obtained beforehand.

The contents of this book are believed to be correct at the time of
printing. Nevertheless, the publishers cannot be held responsible
for any errors or omissions, or for changes in the details given in
this book, or for the consequences of any reliance on the
information provided by the same. This does not affect your
statutory rights.

Advice, technical or legislative details & suggestions are offered in
good faith. However, the authors expressly disclaim any liability
arising from these. Please do your own research prior to
undertaking any course of action suggested or implied herein.

Stories and names may have been anonymised or fictionalised for
privacy reasons. No similarity to any person should be inferred.
Used with express permission.

Thank You

We've so enjoyed sharing all our experiences of campervanning in this book.

Even more, it's been an absolute delight to hear and to relay the tales from the Open Road which have come from fellow-travellers, many of whom have become our clients in recent years. We dare not list them, for fear of missing someone - you know who you are. Thanks for being part of our journey, for your stories and pictures, and support too.

We offer this book to you, our reader, with the hope that it will inspire you to join the growing band of campervan owners, and experience firsthand what all the 'fun' is about...

Daniel & Rebekah

Contents

Your adventure starts here   9

The maiden voyage   15

Where to go in your campervan   27

Wild camping & festivals   42

Longer UK stays   54

To Europe and beyond   68

Try something new   81

Maximum campervan storage   94

Micro living: how to love life on 4 wheels   106

Campervan cuisine   119

Family first: making memories to last a lifetime   127

Canine capers   136

Maintenance made simple   147

Choosing the right campervan for you   159

Travellers' tales: stories from the open road   172

Let your adventures begin   187

About the authors

Daniel and Rebekah Lopez-Ferreiro first discovered campervans as their young family began to grow. Holidays were becoming expensive and travelling was tricky. Country girl Rebekah was certain that a campervan was the perfect solution; Daniel had never been camping as a child, so he wasn't so sure. In the end he agreed to try a trailer tent.

Daniel loved it; breathing in the fresh air, chatting to other campers, this was the good life. They traded up to a caravan, but still watched campervan owners enviously - it looked so easy. With no hitching up, towing or winding of corner steadies, the smart campervan owners were relaxing with a glass of wine, long before Daniel and Rebekah had finished setting up camp.

The couple bought a campervan and travelled all over England, Wales, France and Spain, having so much fun and creating priceless memories. Most of what they needed lived in the campervan, so whenever Daniel could take time out from his heating and plumbing business, they'd just pick a destination and go. The children loved the campervan lifestyle, too.

Soon, Daniel spotted ways he could improve the design of each campervan they bought, and then the van conversions turned into much more than a side project.

Sussex Campervans was born

Daniel and Rebekah started Sussex Campervans at first in rented workshops, then purchasing and relocating to their current woodland location in 2012. They have built hundreds of vehicles for happy customers, who have gone on to enjoy some incredible adventures. You'll meet some of them throughout this book.

Why we love campervans

- Freedom
- Togetherness
- Convenience
- Quality time
- Memories
- Laughter
- Sunsets
- Secluded beaches
- Hidden tracks
- New adventures every day
- Getting away from it all

Chapter 1
Your adventure starts here

Don't call it a dream - make it a plan

We all need something to look forward to, and lots of us really enjoy planning holidays and days out. Perhaps you have already made a 'bucket list' of all the things you'd like to do most in life. Which beautiful cities would you like to visit? Where will you go to find adventures in the wild? Just think how a campervan could make your dreams come true.

Imagine, after a hectic time at work or in your personal life, suddenly you have a free weekend. If you had a campervan sitting there, you could just jump in and drive, stopping on a whim, answerable to no-one.

Today's modern lifestyle can easily turn us all into couch potatoes, as we switch from television screen to computer, or from tablet to phone. As parents and grandparents, aunties and friends, we worry about children's activity levels, often forgetting that they're just copying us. It's up to us to lead the way and show them a healthier way to live. We find that our children thrive when they're whisked away in a campervan, given a chance to try new activities and relax with us.

Soon you'll notch up endless adventures with your kids. Because with your home on wheels (complete with a toilet and a mobile café), you can go anywhere – at a moment's notice, without having to book in advance.

Hit the beach - or head outdoors

Buying a campervan is about so much more than camping holidays.

Don't be surprised if ownership transforms your leisure time - even your life - whether you're retired, single, or raising a family. Practically all hobbies are enhanced by a campervan. If you're into photography, art, history or knitting, you can use the camper when you head off to exhibitions, museums and shows. If you and your children like football, rugby or netball, take the camper along to matches and warm up afterwards with hot soup or even a whole meal in the car park, before going home once the crowds have all gone.

Bird watchers and fishermen often get up early - so why not arrive the night before and be in the right spot at

John & Julie use their CamperCar as a second car and often take it to festivals

Sue & Rick stayed in an Italian olive grove in their Sussex Campervans Paradise Twin

dawn? If you like cycling, the campervan makes a great base vehicle. Some cyclists even head to the Alps to watch the Tour de France cyclists speed past - from the comfort of their camper - or cycle sections of this spectacular route themselves.

A campervan is the perfect vehicle for hikers, mountain bikers, climbers, cavers, anglers, surfers, golfers, writers, painters, stargazers and dog owners.

If we see a superb view when we're out, we just pull over to enjoy it, and brew a cup of tea.

We find that, whether you like quiet time or living life on the edge, this versatile vehicle helps you to enjoy the things you love.

More freedom than you think

As campervan owners, we can enjoy the flexibility and affordability of camping without the hassle of pitching a tent or towing a caravan. We can have the comfort of a B&B without conforming to someone else's rules. Having tasted that freedom, 'package' holidays seem somewhat strait-jacketed.

We don't even need to worry about the rain; we're free to drive on, to find better weather.

With a campervan, it's so easy to get away. Instead of planning ahead and looking for somewhere to stay, we can jump in the van at a moment's notice and explore.

What's more, this isn't a vehicle that sits idle on the driveway for most of the year. Instead, a camper is compact enough to be used as an everyday vehicle. In fact, many people use their campervan as a car because it's not at all cumbersome like the big 'block of flats' type of coachbuilt motorhomes, and is economical too.

With a campervan:
- We can sleep and seat up to five people (depending on the vehicle and layout)
- We can park in a car park or on-street
- We can do the school run
- We can easily maintain and clean it
- We find it does plenty of miles per gallon
- There is enough space inside for the shopping, DIY materials, or even some bicycles.

Take off on a whim; all you need is on board

If you choose to have the interior custom-designed, it should suit you perfectly. It's hard to describe the pleasure people get from having a campervan made to order, with their own choice of colour scheme and fabric textures. Some like to have a practical, wipe-clean interior, especially if they have dogs. Others go for a light, bright and cheerful interior that will make them feel that the weather is sunny, lifting the spirits, even on a cloudy day. Opulent or modern, classy or practical - the choice is yours.

Life without limits

So, how do most people use their campers? The answers are as varied as the individuals themselves, but here are a few of the most popular choices.

- For three-week family touring holidays in France
- For quick Friday night getaways to the beach
- To go to festivals, or try wild camping in comfort

That's the beauty of campervanning: there's plenty of choice about how you use it. Once you start, you'll be hooked.

Chapter 2

The maiden voyage: how to have a brilliant first trip

It's hard to describe the rush of emotions you feel when you hold the keys to your new campervan in your hands

I often get emails like this one:

> *"We're on our first journey with 'Maggie', our new campervan. The Champagne is in the fridge and her first proper outing will be to the Grayson Perry exhibition at the Turner Contemporary in Margate. This evening's view is of Hayling Island, where Pete and I are eating fish and chips."*
>
> *Tracey*

For many people, owning a campervan is a long-term dream so it can be an emotional experience. Suddenly all the possibilities can become a reality.

Imagine you have just picked up your campervan.

Before you head off, think about:

- What equipment do you need to buy?
- Where will you go first?

Tracey found the table with the best view...

Packing for adventures

With the huge selection of camping and outdoor goodies available, it's tempting to kit out your new 'freedom machine' to the hilt. We've had to resist that temptation ourselves. While modern campervans are deceptively spacious, it's best to avoid clutter.

You can always ask your campervan converter what essentials they recommend; they may even have a small accessories shop on-site. We'd advise you to spend at least one night getting to know your van before buying too much equipment. Getting accustomed to your space and how to use it is one of the pleasures of your maiden voyage. When you get back, this is the best time to write your wish list of accessories.

Campervan essentials

Here's our checklist of basics for your first trip away.

- **Portable toilet:** most van conversions contain a dedicated locker for your campervan WC

Michael & Jacky's driveaway awning is cosy at night, while their canopy awning is ideal on a hot summer's day

- **An awning:** perfect for creating your own outdoor space on a campsite and for providing shelter if it rains. There are two choices:
  - **Drive-away awnings:** these freestanding tents attach to the awning rail on the sliding door side of your campervan. Leave it on the pitch when you drive out for the day, and it will save your pitch and provide storage for camping chairs and other non-valuables that you wish to leave behind
  - **A pull-out cassette or canopy awning:** permanently attached to the side or back of the campervan, this simple wind-out canopy gives shade and shelter in minutes
- A drinking water container
- **A waste water container:** take a small bowl so you can collect 'grey' water from the sink and tip it down the campsite's grey water drain
- Toilet chemicals
- **Camping toilet roll:** dissolves after use so it won't clog the cassette toilet

Our toilet fits neatly into a cupboard when not in use

Decide where to go

This is the best bit. We don't want to stifle your adventurous nature, but we recommend you start with an 'easy' trip in a new camper. Ideally, plan a weekend fairly close to home at first, rather than spending all day on the road.

This gives you a chance to get used to the new vehicle and its controls. Don't worry if you've never driven a van before. After half an hour or so, you'll have built up your confidence and got used to the 'feel' of it. There is no substitute for getting behind the wheel and heading off.

When we go away, we like to explore the countryside. With a camper, we can make the most of the scenery – in relative luxury – whether it rains or shines. Depending on where you live, you can discover Dartmoor, the Cornish beaches, the Peak District or the Lake District, the Scottish Borders and Highlands, the Cotswolds, the Yorkshire Moors, the Norfolk Broads – just to name a few. (Your holiday list is growing, isn't it?) In addition, there are countless National Parks to explore, as well as National Trust properties and English Heritage sites to stoke your curiosity.

Where to stay

Here's an overview of places to stay in a camper.

Campsites

There are thousands to choose from - from simple farm campsites with basic facilities, to luxurious commercial campsites with wondrous washrooms, swimming pools, takeaway food outlets, licensed club houses and on-site family entertainment. There are also 'adults only' campsites, for those who want more peace and quiet.

The club sites (below) are well maintained, secure, ruled by wardens and mainly located in rural beauty spots and popular holiday destinations. We use Google or TripAdvisor to find campsites in the area we're visiting - and we do read the reviews online. Buying a campsite guidebook is good holiday reading too. Many campsites have a dog walking area, as well as a shop for essentials.

- The Camping and Caravanning Club
  www.campingandcaravanningclub.co.uk
- The Caravan and Motorhome Club
  www.caravanclub.co.uk
- Camping in the Forest
  www.campingintheforest.co.uk
- The Motor Caravanners' Club, exclusive to campervans and motorhomes
  www.themotorcaravannersclub.co.uk

Street parking

In towns, we look out for parking meters and notices about local parking restrictions. Otherwise (as a general rule) it's not illegal to park up for the night and sleep on-street in the campervan. In our experience, if you 'leave only footprints and take nothing but photographs and good memories', people are rarely bothered. Subtlety is the key, so we park as far away from houses as possible and don't play loud music or put the awning up. If there are only two of us in the camper, we can leave the pop-top down at night. We close the curtains, especially when the light is on inside the camper. Spending a night here and a night there is a great low-key way of exploring all over the country.

Wild camping

It's possible to get off the beaten track and camp in the wilderness. Technically all land in England, Wales and Northern Ireland belongs to somebody, so we do ask the landowner's permission before camping overnight, if we can. There are exceptions - for instance some of the unenclosed land in the Dartmoor National Park - and the wilds of Scotland - where you're allowed to camp responsibly. We just watch out for any signs in car parks, since these may have restrictions. If you're going to Scotland you can find useful information on the Scottish Outdoor Access Code on the website *www.visitscotland.com*. If you're worried about it, go

semi-wild, by using the five-van CL and CS sites licensed by the Caravan and Motorhome Club, the Motor Caravanners' Club and the Camping and Caravanning Club.

Free camping

It may be possible to camp on private land if you have permission from the landowner. Some supermarkets used to turn a blind eye, but now the big ones have cameras to record you if you're staying too long. Motorway Service Stations charge quite a lot for long stays. As ever, we just look out for signs in the car parks.

Aires

We love the fact that many European countries have a network of Aires de Service. These are cheap or free casual campsites for campervans and motorhomes, where we can get fresh water, dispose of waste, and usually stay overnight. These are popular particularly France, but also Spain and Portugal. Google or TripAdvisor will find them for you, or you can buy a guidebook: *www.alltheaires.com*.

Chris & Steph sent us this picture from their stop at an Aire in France

ACSI Camping Card

This discount scheme works in thousands of campsites across Europe, but not in July or August - and you can buy the book from the UK agent: www.vicariousbooks.co.uk

France Passion

This book and vignette allows you to stay for up to 24 hours in your self-contained campervan on the scheme's farms, vineyards and farm shops. In return they hope you will buy their delicious olive oil, cheeses, wines, organic fruit and vegetables, cured meats, honey, foie gras, and other gastronomic delights... Well, it would be rude not to. Visit www.france-passion.com/en

Britstops

Similar to the France Passion Scheme, Britstops gives lists of free campervan stopovers at farm shops, pubs, vineyards and other interesting locations around Britain - www.britstops.com.

Lay-bys

Most A-roads have lay-bys so that all drivers, not just lorry drivers, can stop for a snooze. Some have toilets and are a little set back from the road. If you find a good one, mark it on the map for next time.

On Facebook there are lively campervan community pages that you can join, so you can ask for recommendations from other people.

What to do when you arrive

When we arrive at a campsite, we always park at reception and say 'hello' to the owner or warden. Campsites have different check-in times, but it's best to arrive from 2-6pm. If we're running late, we phone to ask how to check in after hours - they might be a bit grumpy if you keep them waiting for their dinner.

Ask to see the pitches before choosing one, rather than picking from the campsite map.

We like to choose a pitch with:

- Good views
- Friendly fellow campers

- A short walk to the facilities
- A good, flat hardstanding

A hardstanding pitch is ideal for campervans - it should be flat, so there's no need to drive two wheels onto levelling blocks to stop yourself rolling out of bed. It won't get muddy if it rains, either, so that minimises the risk of getting stuck.

Pitch up and relax

Park the campervan within reach of the electric hook-up post, facing the best views - or reverse onto the pitch if

Willow the dog enjoys sunbathing on Bobbie's grassy pitch

it's a Caravan and Motorhome Club site. We leave more space on the side with the habitation door, so that there's room for our camping chairs and awning. Next we hook up the electrics (if available), fill up our water container, lift the pop-top roof and put the kettle on. That's it - we're on holiday.

From bed to driving in minutes

In the morning, simply fold away the bed to put the van into day mode. Wind in the awning (if it's a pull-out one) and ensure everything is secured inside the vehicle. If it's a driveaway awning, just detach it from the camper's awning rail and leave it up on the pitch for the day. Unplug the electric hook-up cable, coil it and put it in the back of the camper. Switch off the gas, bring the pop-top roof down and use the clips or straps to fasten it securely. Then we're free to drive off and explore.

What next?

The first trip is all about getting to know the van and how to make the most of it. As soon as you get home you'll probably be planning your next trip away.

Like many people, Bill & Elsa had only driven cars before

"I'd never driven a van before, so I imagined it would be clunky and awkward - even hard to manoeuvre, but I was wrong. Instead, the vehicle we chose was comfortable and I quickly adjusted to the size and placement of the controls. I liked having a higher vantage point on the road. I was also surprised that the vehicle wasn't a lot bigger than a large car. My wife Elsa liked it, too.

"We enjoy our campervan enormously and use it a lot to explore the UK. We love all the stretches of Heritage Coast around the country. It's fantastic to park up and take in the spectacular views over a cup of tea.

"With a campervan it means we're no longer restricted to summer holidays, or day trips - there was always the risk of experiencing wet weekends in our tent. Now we can explore further afield, in comfort.

"Recently we headed to the north Cornish coast, where the beaches and cliff walks are spectacular. We're also planning to visit the Suffolk and Norfolk coast. It's just so much easier with our campervan. We have bought a Britstops Guide full of interesting and unusual places to spend the night, and we like getting ideas from other people, too.

"Our campervan has made us more adventurous and ready to try new things. For instance, we've found out how much we enjoy sleeping under the stars. I never realised how amazing and magnificent the night sky could be when you're away from all the light pollution of towns and cities.

"We've even been able to spend more time with our niece's children. They love staying in our campervan and we've taken them away with us on a number of occasions now. We would never have been able to do this before.

"There's still so much to do and explore. We've not been to Europe yet - but I'm sure we will. For now we're making the most of what's here in the UK."

Bill & Elsa use their Manhattan MPV all year round, and often enjoy family trips away

When the Fry family collected their Manhattan MPV, their first stop was the Isle of Wight

"For our first weekend away on our campervan we took a trip to the Isle of Wight and enjoyed dramatic skies at The Needles. We have learnt that you cannot do without a roll of black bin liners when it's raining (for all those muddy and wet items) and that there is more than enough cupboard space for a family.

"We also discovered that if you need your morning cuppa to wake up, then it is worth making sure everything is on the bench the night before. There is nothing worse than trying to locate the teabags while you're half awake, with a grunting partner beside you on the Rock 'n' Roll bed."

The Frys sent us a photo of this striking sunset from their trip

Chapter 3

Where to go in your campervan

Every weekend can bring a new adventure in your camper – even if it's just a posh picnic at the beach

Day trips

As campervan owners we are the envy of other day trippers, because everything is easier and more fun.

Beach days

While others have sand in their food, and turn pink behind a windbreak, we can step inside the camper to dry off and change after a good swim, to brew tea, and find shelter from the elements. Like many other families with little children, we love having somewhere comfy for them to have a nap away from the hot sun, when it all gets too much.

Journeys with kids

As all parents know, children get bored when you're driving - but we find we can keep them entertained for longer in a campervan. We keep separate toys, games and colouring books in the camper and put them in a tray on a non-slip mat on the table.

Traffic queues with no stress

School holiday traffic jams have to be seen to be believed. Once we were stuck in a big hold-up on the M1 for three hours. Eventually the police explained that the motorway was closed. While all the car travellers were getting out of their vehicles in frustration, we jumped into the back of the van for a cuppa, and I made a meal. It took some stress out of an awful situation.

Public inconveniences

You need never queue for a public toilet again when you have a portable WC on board - it's a little thing but it makes me smile, every time.

Hiker's retreat

There's no need to cut the day short after a long walk - we like to enjoy the view for a bit longer, while eating, drinking or napping in the campervan.

Beach days are effortless with a camper, as Manhattan MPV owners Bill & Elsa demonstrate

Hot drinks at cool prices

A hot cup of something is an essential part of any day trip - and with a well stocked campervan we can have a hot drink anywhere, anytime. It's so handy.

Posh picnics are on the menu

Gone are the days of soggy sandwiches and a bag of crisps for lunch. We can enjoy fresh salads, yogurts, hot soups, stir-fries, pasta, cold drinks and even fresh strawberries and ice cream from the fridge-freezer in the camper. We can sit at the table, too.

The late drive home: cancelled

When we go out for the day, sometimes we might discover there is a big event happening right there in the evening - or the next morning. If so, we might spontaneously decide to stay the night and enjoy it to the full. There is no need to miss out on live music, or fireworks on the beach, or whatever is going on.

We can also enjoy the simpler pleasures of mesmerising sunsets, glorious sunrises, and the thrill of waking up somewhere new. It's great.

National Trust and English Heritage

Many campervan owners get more value from their National Trust or English Heritage membership, by aiming for beauty spots and stately homes as the lunch stops on longer journeys. It's great to stretch your legs in a beautiful location.

Country parks, wildlife reserves, and special events

From the comfortable base of the campervan, we like to explore wildlife reserves, seasonal markets, food festivals and special events. Destinations like these have plenty of parking and we can make a meal in the campervan to avoid the queues.

Hobbies galore

A campervan makes hobbies a lot more fun. Do you like to surf, fish, ski, write, sail, cycle, or go walking? Maybe you're a stargazer, artist or photographer? Now:

- You can eat, sleep, and relax in comfort
- Your camper makes a good changing room
- You have a cosy place to meet friends

Sophie's family use their camper as an everyday vehicle

Rest, relax and recuperate

We all lead busy, hectic lives and it's possible to lose sight of the important things such as family time, freedom, making new memories and having fun together. With a campervan, you can escape regularly and at a moment's notice.

With all you need packed into your camper, it's so easy to spend quality time away – without breaking the bank. Even if you simply go for a drive and eat a meal somewhere beautiful, it's a lot more fun than grabbing a TV dinner. By keeping it stocked and ready, you can be spontaneous and zoom off at the drop of a hat.

A new environment can give you a fresh perspective. Away from routine, you can let go of the things that may trouble you. Frequent short breaks can help you relax both your mind and your body.

Longer campervan holidays are even better.

Customised to suit the activity

With a bespoke campervan you can customise the layout to suit the hobby. For example you could:

- Ask for an extra table

- Specify storage for golf clubs

- Ask for an access hatch for storing skis, fishing rods, or climbing gear, from behind the rear bed through to the locker beneath

- Request roof rails on top of the pop-top, for surfboards and kayaks

- Choose a tow bar or bike rack for the back

- Have extra lighting and power for your hobbies

Imagine escaping somewhere remote - far away from it all. You've given yourself permission to do your own thing - whatever it may be.

- Chill out with a book or magazine

- Enjoy doing puzzles or crafts

- Find a captivating view, photograph it, paint it or just look at it

- Just drive. Follow your nose and see where you end up

- Watch the sunrise or the sunset

- Have an early morning brew on your campervan steps

- Sleep in (if your kids allow you to)

- Cook marshmallows over a barbecue or camp fire

- Take a stroll on a deserted beach

- Let go and truly relax

Bill & Elsa sent us this photo from a vineyard in France

A campervan allows people to enjoy fresh air and the great outdoors more easily. The camper is the perfect base for discovering our natural surroundings. You can walk along windswept cliffs, sunbathe on sandy beaches, stroll beside reservoirs, or walk through forests - the camper is your passport to the natural world.

You're part of the natural world

There's something sublime about being in nature. When you switch off your phone and disconnect from the internet, you can tune in to another rhythm - running water, lapping waves, the wind rustling through the trees, or the sound of birds high above - nature's orchestra is good for the soul. It can calm you.

Lots of us spend too long slouched over a computer at work, or a tablet or phone at other times. Our bodies are designed to move - so walking in the countryside can make you feel great.

It may be compact, but a campervan kitchen is surprisingly versatile. There are so many delicious and healthy recipes that you can prepare on two rings.

Mel saw this stunning skyline in the French countryside

Even a one-day break will energise you so you can sail through another working week, while you plan your next great escape.

Mini breaks and weekenders

One of the biggest benefits a modern van conversion has over a coachbuilt model is its nimbleness. With a footprint not dissimilar to a large car, their size makes them easy to drive and park. These vehicles are economical too. In fact, you'll be surprised at the fuel economy many campervans offer nowadays.

Clunkiness and fuel costs help to explain why lots of larger motorhomes sit idly on the drive for big chunks of the year. But with a campervan, you can use it as often as you like.

Here are some ideas:

Spontaneous breaks
If you keep your campervan stocked up with all the essentials, you can get away at a moment's notice without booking. Simply load any perishables into your fridge/freezer, pack a few clothes, fill up your water container and you're ready to go.

Extended day trips
The range of a day trip in a car is restricted because you have to come home at the end of the day. Not so in a campervan - just stay over.

Culture and city breaks
Winter is the ideal time for city breaks, art galleries, exhibitions, theatre trips, music gigs and fine dining... perhaps a little shopping, too. We like to find a campsite near the venue, or on a good train route into the city. It's good to make the most of tourist leaflet offers and train companies' 'two for one' ticket deals.

Visits to friends and family
It's easy to visit people without imposing on them - simply sleep in your campervan.

Weddings
Parking near the wedding venue means you'll have no worries about getting back to your accommodation afterwards - or hotel bills.

Theme parks
You can get more from your visit to Longleat Safari Park, Alton Towers, Poultons, and other theme parks, when you have a campervan. Now you can make the most of their great value two-day tickets by staying somewhere close by without the expense of staying in a hotel or

Steve & Birgit's CamperCar helps them climb mountains

Steve & Birgit found snow in the Scottish mountains

Birgit explains, "I've pretty much gone camping all my life. There was even a time when I sold my house, bought a van, and spent two years climbing - because I had lots of mountains to climb.

"Spending a lot of money and ending up with the wrong van wasn't an option for us - so after much research, two visits to motorhome shows, poking around dozens of different vans and talking to many van people - we decided that the NV200 CamperCar from Sussex Campervans was the one for us.

"We use our CamperCar just about every weekend and holiday and it's my everyday vehicle, too. It's already done 24,000 problem-free miles since we bought it in August 2015 and I've spent 56 nights sleeping in it - the longest single trip being 18 days. Plus, we've got another 30 van nights scheduled over the next few months. We keep setting ourselves more challenges and one adventure always leads to another one.

"It's a great vehicle to drive, both in town and at speed on the motorway. More importantly for me, it copes with the steep, narrow single track roads of the Welsh mountains and North-West Scotland, where it tucks very neatly into the single passing places with ease."

Extreme sports challenges

"We spend a lot of time in these parts of the country. I've already climbed all the mountains over 3000 ft in Scotland, England, Ireland and Wales, and everything over 2,000 ft in England and Wales. I've also run mountain marathons, and a van is great to use as a base camp for these type of events. It's a never-ending journey, and I love it. I love reaching a new summit, discovering a new view, and being at one with nature. Our current project is to climb the highest hill in each of the 91 historic counties of Great Britain - from Cornwall and Kent to Orkney and Shetland - it's a challenge that seems to have been designed just for the pleasure of travelling around and living in our CamperCar.

"Our campervan gives us a sense of freedom. It's like a tortoise shell - you take it everywhere you go, so you always have a dry bed, and it's surprising how little you need once you're on the road.

"The layout of our CamperCar can easily accommodate all our specialist climbing gear - and there's a lot of it. From ropes to crampons, skis and survival gear, everything has its place. My skis can even slide in neatly under the seats from the back. We keep our bag of dry clothes under the front half of the back seat, all the things we need for overnight in stowage net bags in the side locker and all our hill gear under the rear part of the back seat. When other climbers look inside our van, they're amazed at how much kit we can fit in and how well it all works."

It's weathered the storms

Birgit has lived in a campervan in all weathers. She says, "I remember one time in Scotland the temperature plummeted to -17°C. We survived! During storms we tend to keep the pop-top down, but even then there's still plenty of room to chill out, eat, drink, read, snooze, and watch the iPlayer. It is better than going to the pub.

"I get envious looks from soggy tent campers and compliments from other campervan people (and wannabe campervan people), who come round for a nosy peek and who are amazed at how well the Sussex-built van looks, how well it's equipped and how well it performs 'in the field'.

"Our CamperCar was a good choice - and it is now very much part of our way of life, and we use it as much as we can. The van and its layout works brilliantly for me. I love having a dry space to relax in with a nice hot cup of tea after a long walk. It's so much better than going away with just a tent."

Birgit uses the CamperCar as her base for mountain marathons

Brian walks Bailey the dog, and reads the morning papers every day in his Manhattan campervan

"Right from the start I used my campervan lots because it's become my main vehicle - and it's so flexible. My black Labrador, Bailey, loves it almost as much as I do. He comes with me everywhere in the campervan. He loves sitting on his cushion bed, and I always have a struggle to tempt him out when we get home, because he doesn't want to leave.

"Bailey and I have got into a really nice routine. Every morning, we drive to Burnham Beeches, near Farnham in Surrey, for a lovely walk through the beech woods. Bailey loves it. I park up under the trees and after an hour or so we'll head back to the van for a nice hot cup of tea and toast for me, and plenty of water and dog food for Bailey. I have bought a brilliant pyramid toaster, that sits on top of the gas ring and works perfectly. With breakfast made, I sit back and read the morning papers until I fancy going home. This is the life of retirement!

"I have been further afield, too. Our favourite trip so far was when we went to North Cornwall for a wedding. The wedding was held in a field in Delabole, a village between the coast and Camelford. It's not far from King Arthur's Tintagel and Port Isaac - of TV's Doc Martin fame - and we came through Launceston on the way.

"The other guests were staying in some big teepees. Unfortunately, it rained on the first night, but that didn't bother us. We simply put on the heater. The wedding guests staying in the teepees got rather damp, but Mary, Bailey and I were lovely and snug in our warm campervan.

"We have lots more adventures planned and we are really looking forward to taking the grandchildren to the sandy beach at West Wittering, in Sussex, in the summer. Children love campervans and it's going to be so lovely to spend the time with them."

Brian & Bailey enjoy a cuppa in their Manhattan campervan after their walk

Holidays in France were suddenly almost as easy as trips to the local garden centre in Sussex, for Barry and Carol

Barry and Carol live in Sussex, and Carol was the driving force behind getting a campervan. She says, "I was inspired to get a campervan, because I could see what fun other members of Barry's family were enjoying in theirs. I didn't want the vehicle just for holidays and day trips. Instead, I was looking for an all-year-round, everyday vehicle, which would be easy to park in town.

"I was keen to find out if a campervan could be driven and used during non-camping times. So I actually visited some van converters, without telling Barry, to see what was available.

"I was really delighted with what I found. It was clear to me that a campervan conversion was a lot more versatile than I'd first realised and I could see that we'd get a lot of use out of it - for pleasure and for practical stuff. In the end Barry and I ordered our 'built to order' bespoke Nissan NV200 CamperCar."

Barry says, "For our first trip away, we took the Newhaven/Dieppe ferry, before driving down to La Rochelle, in South-West France. It was a long drive, but so beautiful and enjoyable in our campervan. We could pull over whenever we wanted to have a break, a cup of tea, and stretch our legs.

"We had been on at least six car driving holidays in France, the furthest being to Provence. However, we found driving the CamperCar in France was as easy as driving our Toyota Corolla."

Freedom to roam

"We loved the freedom of just driving from place to place with no plan. There was so much to see and discover and so many memories to bring home. From La Rochelle, we went across the bridge to the Île de Ré, where we drank Champagne and sampled the island's famous oysters.

"The joy of the CamperCar was having everything we needed - whenever we needed it. One extra came in very handy - a pop-up toilet tent! While there is room in the vehicle to use the toilet, we preferred to put it outside for privacy. The tent had other uses too. When we were on a campsite we tended to use the on-site facilities, so the toilet tent became a dressing room. We even used it to store things or reserve our pitch when we were out for the day. We've loved our campervan and put it to brilliant use."

Trading up to a Paradise

Now, after three years of fun, Barry and Carol have traded in their CamperCar and ordered a Paradise Compact. It's based on a short wheelbase Renault Trafic, so it's a slightly larger campervan, offering them a good-size kitchen at the rear, and a choice of twin single beds or a king-size double bed in the front. It's a beautiful camper, and Barry and Carol say they are looking forward to their new adventures.

Barry & Carol love touring Europe in their camper

Chapter 4

Wild camping & festivals

Wild camping

One of the biggest draws of the campervan lifestyle is the freedom. With everything you need in the back of your van you can just jump in and drive and see where you end up. Get away from the crowds, and you may stumble upon a deserted beach, a beautiful undisturbed moorland view, or a lake that takes your breath away.

If parking is permitted, you can even stay the night there. This is wild camping at its best – the chance to enjoy the undisturbed wilderness, starlit skies, sunrises and sunsets and be at peace with nature.

It's the ultimate escape.

Many people do feel a little nervous about wild camping - because it's inevitably remote. (Have you ever noticed how a place can feel very different after dark?) Campers can also get confused about what is and isn't permitted.

Rules as to where you can park your campervan overnight vary from country to country. So before you head off do a little research online, to minimise the chance that you'll be asked to move on, in the middle of the night.

To give you an idea, you need permission from the landowner in England (every acre of England is owned by someone – whether it's a private person, a company, or a public body). So while you can park in lay-bys and beside the roads (unless there is a sign forbidding overnight stays), you can't pull over and set up camp anywhere you like.

The National Trust and Forestry Commission do not permit overnight camping on their land. However, you can ask farmers and other landowners for permission to park up. Many are very accommodating - especially if you treat their land with respect.

Another option is to stay in car parks and beside the road. Do your research and you might find a perfect spot. For example, there's a lovely beach near to where we live that we often visit and camp overnight. It's blissful - especially the following morning when the kids jump out of the van after a good night's sleep and race onto the sand. Happy days!

Scotland is different from England. You have much more freedom to camp up in remote locations and get off the beaten track. The Scottish scenery is stunning, too. So if you head north of the border you could find a perfect spot with a mountain view, or park up near a lake and enjoy a glass of whisky.

You can find more information about wild camping in Scotland at:

www.visitscotland.com/accommodation/caravan-camping/wild-camping

One more thing... if you can't find anywhere remote to park free of charge, remember there are many campsites offering a wild camping experience.

Wild camping considerations

Free camping is all about confidence. Here are some pointers to ensure you have a brilliant time in the wild.

Safety and security

As wild camping is often associated with remote places, you need to be safety and security conscious. For example you want to avoid areas with a busy night community. Just use your instincts. When you spot somewhere that looks perfect, take a few moments to get a sense of how you feel. If you don't feel comfortable there, move on. Similarly, the atmosphere of a location can change as the sun goes down. A place that felt brilliant at midday can be eerie at dusk. Don't feel you have to stick it out.

Permission

We try to check the local laws, so we don't park if there are signs saying that overnight camping is not allowed, and if we want to stay on private land, where possible, we try to seek permission from the owner.

Keep a low profile

It's wise not to camp in sight of houses, as you're likely to draw attention and possibly even a visit from the police. When we're wild camping, we don't set up a busy camp, and we keep the awning tucked away. While it's okay to sit outside on chairs, we keep everything else inside, to remain inconspicuous. That way you are less likely to get asked to move on. We make sure we're not blocking tracks, field gateways or driveways.

Ready to drive

While the idea of opening a bottle of wine and relaxing to the sounds and sights of nature is hugely appealing to many wild campers, make sure at least one driver is available. If you do get asked to move on, you can drive away safely - and legally.

Water

Take sufficient fresh water for your overnight stay, or a means of purifying water.

Waste

Be sensitive when disposing of your grey water (from washing, dishes and cleaning teeth). Mostly you can use it to water the bushes, but where possible use environmentally friendly washing-up liquid to minimise the impact on local wildlife.

Check for firm ground and tides

Park on a nice, firm base, so you won't get stuck in the mud. Level ground is preferable, to prevent funny, uncomfortable sleeping positions. Some of the most idyllic wild camping spots are beside water. A friend once parked her campervan on Bettystown beach, near Dublin, for a quick post-ferry sleep. When she woke up, the other vehicles had driven away, and the tide was coming in fast. Other parking areas to avoid at high tide include Twickenham Riverside in West London, and Bosham Harbour near Chichester.

Rubbish

Keep your rubbish inside (not under) the camper, as it can attract badgers, foxes and other wildlife to tear it open in search of food.

Toilet stuff

If you use your onboard cassette toilet, take all waste with you and empty it responsibly. If you don't have a toilet and want to go in the wilds, take a trowel so that you can cover your waste with soil.

Be extra considerate after dark

Keep your noise level to a minimum and avoid playing loud music so as not to trouble the local residents.

Remember the wild campervanning rule: *Arrive with everything you need and leave nothing behind.*

We could never get bored with waking up and looking out to sea – what a view!

Festival fun

There are so many interesting and unusual festivals held every year, all around the world. There are religious camps and music festivals, art, comedy and theatre gatherings, spectacular balloon festivals, carnival weeks, food and drink events, and more.

Plenty of these events are expecting campervans to turn up, because many people realise that this is the way to enjoy festivals in style.

Once you have your first campervan you may even book your first festival, safe in the knowledge that you won't have to deal with soggy tents and the event's clogged up toilets.

Adrian enjoys cooking up a feast at VW campervan festivals

Campervans and music are a match made in heaven

Adrian is a seasoned festival-goer. He says, "During the festival season, I'll take my V-Dub campervan to events like Camper Jam and Busfest." Camper Jam is the family VW camper gathering in Shropshire, while Busfest is the 'world's largest VW Transporter Show' in Malvern.

"I love the atmosphere and the entertainment," says Adrian. "If you've never taken a campervan to a music festival before, don't be surprised if your first time becomes the first of many."

Why take a campervan to music festivals, instead of a lightweight tent?

"There are so many reasons why I love my campervan," says Adrian. "Night times tend to be a lot quieter, because you can shut the door when you want to sleep. It's a comfortable bed, and if it rains, there's no problem. The van is always warm and cosy and there's no need to endure a soggy sleeping bag or the cold ground underneath you in a tent. If it's really hot, I love that I can escape to the cool shade of my campervan. Perhaps best of all, there's a portable toilet on board."

Adrian has some good advice for new festival goers. He says, "At a festival, campervans often have to park a bit further away from the action (but that's rarely a big deal). There are usually fewer spaces designated for campervans so if I know it's going to be a busy event then I'll make sure I get there early so I can bag a good spot for myself and my friends.

"I've made my best friends through owning a Volkswagen campervan and taking it to the V-Dub group events. It's great travelling in a group with like-minded people. We have so much fun. Often we'll rock up to a campsite, cook outdoors together, and chat into the night over a few drinks. I've had really enjoyable holidays and weekends and made lifelong friendships by going away with my campervan."

Our own first wild camping experience - an impromptu decision left us itching for more...

On one trip, we were driving through northern Spain when we stumbled upon the most beautiful deserted beach. Our children had discovered a cave. The sand was silky white and the beach was littered with interesting shells to collect. The beach was so still and peaceful. It was mesmerizing.

We noticed a German campervan had parked up for the night in the sandy/grassy car park. It was all the reassurance we needed to experience wild camping for the first time. We had enough food and water on board so there was nothing to stop us.

It was perfect watching the sunset on the still sea, while the fishing boats sailed towards the horizon in search of their night's catch. As it got darker, the lighthouse light began blinking in the distance and the twinkling stars filled the sky. Everyone went to sleep happily. Although I was sure someone would knock on the door in the night and ask us to move on – they didn't.

Everyone enjoyed a good night's sleep and after a relaxing breakfast, with the sound of the sea lapping just a few metres away, it was time to move on to our next stop.

And that was it... Our appetite for wild camping had started. The sentiment of 'born to be wild' springs to mind whenever I remember some of the remote spots we've discovered. It's a unique experience and quite different to a noisy campsite. The silence and blackness of a remote location is something else. Actually, from time to time, it's good to be alone.

Imagine waking up and finding yourself surrounded...

Birgit says "I've done a lot of wild camping. I've found some awesome campsites over the years. I look for somewhere sheltered, so we don't get blown about by the weather. Preferably somewhere with a good view.

"I've had some crazy experiences over the years. There was the time when we were climbing in the Southern Cairngorms. I remember waking up to find ourselves surrounded by Royal Marines (with guns and full Arctic camouflage) guarding our van as a training exercise. That was fairly intimidating, but memorable."

Musical John and yoga teacher Julie love their CamperCar, which they've christened Beano

"We took delivery of our lovely NV200 campervan less than a year ago and we absolutely love it! In fact we almost "fight" over who's turn it is to drive it as we use it as our second car all the time," says John.

"When we saw the number plate BNO, we looked at each other and both said "Beano" at the same time. So that was it! It's bright red which really stands out and draws lots of comments and jealous looks when we pull up on a campsite.

"I play a lot of music and my wife Julie is a yoga teacher, so we put a few discreet decals on the silver stripe that Sussex Campervans put on for us. Musical notes for me and small yoga symbol, which says 'Just Breathe' on the back panel.

"Also the lovely people at Sussex Campervans fixed up a simple but effective little extra for me. I now have special straps inside and under the roof panel which comfortably houses my travel guitar. So when we stop for the evening, I'm generally entertaining the missus with a few songs whilst she's usually knitting something for the many grandchildren now coming on the scene!

"We've had Beano for less than a year, but already have been on trips to Cornwall, Dorset and Norfolk. We've also been to a couple of festivals with it."

They added their own custom decals to match their hobbies

John and Julie can now enjoy their trips in style

Chapter 5

Longer UK stays

In addition to short breaks, I'm sure you'll be itching to enjoy extended breaks with your campervan

Cornish coves are just waiting to be explored...

Yes, a campervan is perfect for a summer holiday – with kids, your partner, friends, or solo.

With a campervan, you can begin to discover the variety and beauty of the British Isles. From the sandy beaches of Cornwall, to the rolling hills and moors of Somerset, to the craggy Munro Mountains of Scotland, you'll find yourself spoilt for choice.

Where will you start? How about one of these popular UK holiday spots?

Cornwall

Tucked away in the far south-west of England, Cornwall offers a magnificent selection of sandy beaches, breathtaking coastlines, and thriving fishing villages to explore. From surfing off Newquay beach to hiking the South West Coastal Path, or indulging in the county's famous Cornish pasties and cream teas, Cornwall is an idyllic county to explore with your campervan.

Park up for Lynton and Lynmouth's cliff railway

Home to the world famous Eden Project and Tintagel Castle - where King Arthur grew up, according to legend. Cornwall offers a wealth of different types of campsites, remote hideaways, cliffs, sandy beaches and many tourist attractions.

Devon

Home to The English Riviera, great cities such as Plymouth and Exeter, and family-friendly beaches, Devon has something for everyone. Visit Dartmoor and Exmoor National Parks in Devon, with rugged landscapes, imposing tors, hardy ponies, red deer and wild goats in the awe-inspiring wilderness.

The moors are perfect places to get off the beaten track and escape to somewhere remote. There are many campsites, where you can spend the night in the wilderness. We've toured Devon and visited Dartmoor by camper - we loved getting close to the ponies.

Exmoor

Spanning Devon and Somerset, Exmoor is also an International Dark Sky reserve, which makes it a perfect spot for some stargazing, even with a naked eye. You'll also discover signs of civilisation from long ago, with ruined walls, burial mounds and standing stones.

Visit Plymouth and Exeter in Devon for a spot of retail therapy, or Lynton and Lynmouth for fresh fish and chips and a cliff railway. You can also visit Paignton and Dartmoor Zoo. Finally, Devon has many stunning beaches, farm parks, steam railways and tourist attractions, making it a brilliant all round holiday destination.

Dorset and the Jurassic Coast

The Jurassic Coast is a UNESCO World Heritage Site that stretches from East Devon to Dorset. The exquisite geological structures mean that you can almost walk back in time and you might even discover a few fossils of your own in the fallen rocks on the beach (a great activity to do with children). Charmouth beach has plenty of parking and is a brilliant place to hunt for fossils - even if you're a complete amateur.

Some of the geological highlights in the West Country include the limestone arch of Durdle Door, the

There are good campsites near to Dorset's Durdle Door

windswept shingle strand of Chesil Beach, and the squat sea stacks at Ladram Bay, near Sidmouth. And with miles of footpaths, breathtaking coastal views, and scenic drives, your campervan is the perfect vehicle to use to take in the glory of this important destination.

The Isle of Wight

Just a short ferry hop across the Solent and you'll find yourself on England's largest island. With over 60 miles of beaches to explore, you can try rock pooling, swimming, sunbathing, and all kinds of watersports. Remember to check out The Needles, the chalk rocks surrounded by sea at the south-west tip of the island. This natural geological structure is perhaps the most iconic image of this interesting island.

You can walk or take the chairlift down to the beach and marvel at Alum Bay's multi-coloured sandstone cliffs. There are also fairground rides and attractions for children here, and a chance to look inside The Battery - one of England's key defensive outposts in World War II. In addition, there's Carisbrooke Castle, Queen Victoria's beloved Osborne House, the sailing Mecca of Cowes,

genteel coastal paths, bridleways, and cycle tracks galore. The Isle of Wight is a great destination for all age groups, and with so many excellent campsites here, you'll be spoilt for choice.

The Cotswolds

Incorporating major locations such as Gloucester, Bath, Tewksbury, and Cheltenham, this picturesque area is characterised by its rolling hills or 'wolds'. An outdoor paradise, this Area of Outstanding Natural Beauty has thousands of miles of footpaths – perfect for hiking through ancient woodland, wildflower meadows, and delightful valleys. Cyclists will be just as inspired, with an array of tracks to explore.

The Cotswolds is also home to quintessentially English villages, full of thatched stone cottages, magnificent stately homes, and historic castles – so there's plenty to keep you occupied. And don't forget to take high tea in the Roman Baths in Bath. This well preserved relic allows you to step back in time in the most genteel fashion - see the health-giving spa baths and walk on the same cobblestones as our Roman ancestors.

Visit picture-perfect Bibury in the Cotswolds

The Suffolk Coast

This Area of Outstanding Natural Beauty is a haven for wildlife. You'll even find RSPB Minsmere, a location for BBC TV's Springwatch. There are plenty of sandy beaches, such as Europe's largest spit at Orford Ness, as well as salt marshes, which attract migrating birds. Immortalised by John Constable in The Hay Wain, and other great paintings, the level Suffolk countryside is full of picturesque and fertile arable farms, while the coast also attracts foodies, outdoor enthusiasts, and wildlife fans.

Whether you're tasting local produce bought from the markets, or enjoying the charming seaside towns of Felixstowe and Southwold, or perhaps kayaking down the Alde Estuary, a campervan will help you take in more of this perfect getaway.

Snowdonia National Park

The spectacular coastline and mountains of North Wales draw climbers and walkers all year round. This is the place to walk up Mount Snowdon; at 1,085 metres it's the highest mountain in England and Wales. In summer, you may have a chance to enjoy the breathtaking views from a train window, thanks to the Snowdon Mountain Railway, but reaching this famous peak isn't the only reason to visit this richly diverse region. With campsites galore, you can be comfortable and enjoy hot showers after days out hiking beside lakes and rivers, up mountains, and through gorges.

There are plenty of places to hike and cycle in North Wales, as well as a plethora of other outdoor pursuits to try, for all the family. If you ever tire of the nine mountain ranges, you'll find more than 200 miles of seashore to explore. Snowdonia's sandy beaches, sheltered harbours, ragged cliffs and views of Brunel's bridge to Anglesey will take your breath away.

The North Pennines

Located in the North of England, The North Pennines is an Area of Outstanding Natural Beauty, characterised by high moorland and broad upland dales.

With its panoramic views, stunning natural features, and extensive wild places, this destination is perfect for windswept walks, escaping from society, and indulging

Tranquil Beddgelert is steeped in legend

in all manner of outdoor pursuits. Here, you can try everything from bushcraft to climbing or horse riding.

A haven for wildlife, the North Pennines offers you a chance to walk through hay meadows, wonder at thundering waterfalls, and imagine days gone by, in a landscape shaped by years of lead mining. Due to its remoteness, the North Pennines is also a perfect location for amateur and professional astronomers. There's a choice of official Dark Sky Discovery Sites, from which you can gaze upon the heavens above when the sun goes down. You don't have to stray far from the warmth and comfort of your campervan to do it.

The Lake District

The Lake District is England's largest National Park and is home to England's highest mountain (Scafell Pike) and England's largest lake (Lake Windermere). With plenty of space to explore, you can grab a walking guide and hike for miles.

Of course, this glorious destination is best known for beautiful lakes, of which there are 16 in total. Thanks to the distinctive landscape, you can enjoy scenic boat trips, challenging off-road cycling trails, and dramatic drives. The Lake District has heritage, too. For example, you can step inside children's book author Beatrix Potter's house at Hill Top, or visit Lake Coniston, where Donald Campbell was killed while attempting to beat his own water speed record, and discover the poet William Wordsworth's house in Grasmere.

The Scottish Highlands

Unspoilt and untamed, the mesmerising Scottish Highlands are just magical. Within Britain's largest National Park the landscapes will take your breath away, and the opportunities for exploring the mountains, lochs and fells will keep you occupied for days.

You can climb Ben Nevis, Britain's highest mountain. Away from the mountains you can take a boat trip and hunt for Nessie, the famously elusive Loch Ness Monster. You'll find castles and cathedrals, and with the North Coast 500 route to explore, there are plenty of opportunities to take your campervan right off the beaten track.

The Norfolk Broads

Nestled in the east of the country, the Norfolk Broads are best known for a seemingly endless network of rivers and 'broads' (or lakes). In fact, with seven rivers and 63 lakes it's the UK's largest protected wetland area. While hiring a boat is a great way to explore this spectacular area, a holiday here offers quite a lot more than just boating adventures.

This magnificent wetland area is a haven for birds - there are lots to see and watch. There are also plenty of traditional windmills to discover.

You can explore many market towns and quaint villages if you want to soak up the culture or indulge in a spot of retail therapy. Don't forget the plentiful tracks and trails taking you riverside and beyond - perfect for gentle cycling and hiking on the flat.

Of course a trip to the Broads wouldn't be complete without at least one day on the water. So why not treat yourself to a boat trip? Set off down river and soak up the atmosphere. Alternatively, you could try exploring the Broads by canoe - it's one of the best ways to see this remarkable region. When you're back on dry land, if you don't fancy cooking in your campervan there are plenty of restaurants, bars, cafés, and pubs to suit all tastes in cuisine.

The Brecon Beacons

Perfect for an adventure, the stunning Brecon Beacons National Park, in the southern heart of Wales, is characterised by heather-clad mountains and breathtaking views. Head here if you enjoy such activities as hillwalking, climbing, caving and cycling - and don't forget to breathe in plenty of that pure fresh air. There are activities galore to discover.

You could trek a section of the Beacons Way. This 95-mile route crosses the National Park. Or why not climb South Wales' highest peak, Pen-y-Fan?

You'll find plentiful fishing along the River Usk. How about hiring a mountain bike and striking out on one of the many trails? You can ride a horse, escape into the forests, or explore the waterways by canoe. If you're into the excitement of adrenalin sports, you could even try canyoning. Join a guided tour and you can jump off a

Brecon offers mountains, rivers and bike trails

waterfall and navigate the rapids in the river. Alternatively, explore the beauty underground by visiting Dan yr Ogof, at the National Showcaves Centre for Wales. This impressive 10-mile-long cave system even has an underground river.

The New Forest

The mixed landscape and wild ponies of the New Forest National Park in Southern England are a real draw. On the one hand, you can lose yourself in the highest concentration of ancient trees in Western Europe. You'll discover centuries old oak trees and beech trees. There are even some yews that are believed to be over 1,000 years old.

The New Forest also has a coastal border characterised by mudflats, salt marshes and lagoons, making it a valuable spot for hoards of wildlife. There are countless walking trails to explore and many family-friendly bike routes. The Lymington-Keyhaven Nature Reserve offers fantastic views across the Solent to the Isle of Wight. There are plenty of campsites, and you could even visit Beaulieu Motor Museum and Buckler's Hard.

The Peak District

This glorious region spans Derbyshire, Staffordshire, Cheshire and Yorkshire. It's crowning glory is the Peak District National Park, at the southernmost tip of The Pennines. It is home to moorland, rivers, springs, and endless views.

Explore this stunning region on foot, bike, or horseback. There are lots of car parks dotted throughout the area. How about riding the cable cars at The Heights of Abraham or exploring some of the many caverns and marvelling at the astonishing stalactites and stalagmites.

Northumberland

From the Holy Island of Lindisfarne to a rich array of stately homes and gardens, there's plenty to keep you busy. Northumberland also has a National Park, which is tranquil and beautiful. It's a haven for lovers of outdoor pursuits. There are crags for climbing, dramatic hills and open spaces to discover, and trails to explore, so this location attracts climbers, walkers and cyclists. You'll even spot wild mountain goats showing off their mountaineering skills.

There's spectacular scenery to be found in the hills

Peter & Linda took their Manhattan camper to Snowdon

"We knew Mount Snowdon would be busy later in the day, so we were first in the car park, at dawn, last summer. We walked up the mountain and arrived at the summit by 7.30 am, before the first train came up. It was empty - lovely.

"By the time we'd walked back down the mountain, the car park was full and there were barriers down to stop anyone else getting in. We had just got our timing just right. It's always so nice to come back to the campervan after a walk."

Snowdonia is a popular destination – mountain lovers Steve and Birgit also visited recently in their CamperCar

Jenny has owned her CamperCar for a year, and she's mostly used it for short breaks and archaeological digs

Milo the Border Terrier is sitting comfortably...

She says, "I love my CamperCar with its turquoise and purple seats. I went to Charmouth, Dorset, for two nights when I was learning the ropes in my new campervan. The trip was about 80 per cent successful - the only tricky bit was that one of my two Border Terriers, Gypsy, wanted a wee at 4am. She escaped across the field, pursued by me, in my fleecy pyjamas!

"Then I took the dogs to Borderfest North, at Kingsbury Water Park Camping and Caravan site in the Midlands. For the third trip I went to Wales and took my friend Sally. She slept in the awning and the weather was so bad that it was like a hurricane - the communal gazebo on the campsite blew down, but the driveaway awning that I'd bought with the van stayed up.

"I went to Abinger in Surrey to see an archaeological site and cooked bacon sandwiches for all the people on the dig. They've come to expect it now. I've been out in the camper for plenty of picnics, too.

"For a longer holiday I went to Northumberland, via the Lincolnshire Wolds. The Three Horseshoes Inn at Goulceby near Louth in Lincolnshire let me stay in their car park overnight.

"When I got to Northumberland I stayed at another pub, the Railway Tavern, and the dogs won a fancy dress competition. I dressed Milo up as Fred Flintstone - I tied some leopard print fabric around him and I sewed a bone onto the shoulder. My other dog, Gypsy, wore a frilly dress, and they both won. Most people had bought fancy dress outfits.

"I really loved Northumberland, especially Warkworth Castle and Hermitage, overlooking a river near the coast. The beaches are beautiful. I drove back all in one day, which took seven hours. That's the only thing about travelling solo, it's a bit dangerous to drive such a long way on your own in case you get too tired. This year I will be going to Ironbridge for a holiday, then to Borderfest at Kingsbury Water Park again in May. The CamperCar is very comfortable for me and the dogs. I'm not really a wild camper - I prefer the safety and comforts of campsites."

Jenny's granddaughter loves the CamperCar, too

Chapter 6

To Europe and beyond

A campervan makes exploring further afield a breeze

When heading to Europe, there is no need to squash everything into a suitcase; campervan touring is far more flexible and affordable.

If you're put off by the thought of driving on the 'wrong' side of the road, you needn't be. Sure, those first few minutes off the ferry/shuttle can be a little tense, but you'll be surprised at how quickly you'll acclimatise to a different way of driving. You can even buy a special sticker to fix to your windscreen to remind you to drive on the right as an aid.

With the Channel Tunnel and a choice of ferry crossings to France, Spain, Holland, Belgium, and the Channel Islands, a campervan opens up a whole new world of affordable holidays, with the chance to experience different cultures, cuisine and wine.

Getting there

It's very easy to take your campervan to Europe. Small and compact, your camper will cost less than you think to take through the Channel Tunnel, or on a ferry.

- Eurotunnel (*www.eurotunnel.com*)

  The journey through the Channel Tunnel from Folkstone to Calais is just 35 minutes, making this the fastest way to get to France.
- P&O Ferries (*www.poferries.com*)
- Brittany Ferries (*www.brittany-ferries.co.uk*)
- DFDS (*www.dfdsseaways.co.uk*)

Discounted camping and travel

The good news is that there are several ways to save money on your next European holiday.

Cheaper ferry crossings

Join the Caravan and Motorhome Club (*www.caravanclub.co.uk*) and you can save money on ferry tickets when you book through them.

Site Discount Schemes:

These discount schemes are perfect for low season:

Touring Europe costs less if you use Aires instead of campsites - thanks to Bill & Elsa for this great photo

- Camping Travel Club (Camping Cheque and Holiday Cheque schemes combined). You buy a 'cheque' for a fixed price pitch that's valid on more than 600 campsites in 22 European countries during the low and mid-seasons. Prices in the low season start from just 15-19 euros per night. Visit www.campingtravelclub.com or ring 0033 3 85 72 29 90.

- The CampingCard from ACSI is a similar scheme that also makes off-season camping more affordable. Perfect if you like the freedom of just showing up, your card is valid for immediate discount at over 3000 campsites. In fact, you can save up to 50%. See www.campingcard.co.uk.

- Camping Key Card (CKE) also provides discounts in thousands of sites across Europe (including some during peak season). In addition, your card doubles up as proof of identity in Europe too. This can be handy as many campsites will accept your CKE card instead of your passport at check-in. The card also has some third-party insurance included too. See www.campingkey.com.

Staying abroad

As well as campsites, you and your campervan have other options on the Continent.

Aires

An Aire is a location where campervans can stock up on fresh water, empty waste, and often stay overnight cheaply or free of charge. Some Aires have electric hook-ups and other facilities, too. Aires are an attractive way of travelling from place to place across Europe – just for campervans – no caravans or tents are allowed.

Vicarious Books publish excellent guides to Aires across Europe. You can use Google to find Aires, but books are handy if there's no phone signal - see www.vicarious-shop.com/home

France Passion Scheme

France Passion is a growing network of over 9,500 vineyards, farms, and other spots, which welcome campervan owners to park overnight on their land, free of charge. In return, these hosts will invite you to try their produce in the hope that you'll buy something. We've really enjoyed it.

The France Passion scheme makes it easy to explore rural France and enjoy local delicacies and produce. Stay somewhere safe and enjoy wine tasting, or buy olive oil, local cheeses, pâté de foie gras, honey, fruit and vegetables. Your passport to the scheme is just to buy a France Passion guidebook to find out where the places are. See *www.france-passion.com*

One more thing...

When you are deciding where to go, we recommend that you should check the weather in your chosen destination. In the past we have found that if one part of the coastline is bracing itself for storms, we can change our plan instantly and head in the other direction for a location with better weather.

Visit 'les plus beaux villages de France'

European touring checklist

Packing for an overseas trip needn't be stressful. With a campervan you are far less restricted for space than if you'd flown and had to squeeze everything into a suitcase. Most of what you take will be the same as you need in the UK, but there are some differences.

Before you go it's wise to check the rules of the country you're due to visit. This checklist is a good start, though each European destination has its own subtleties.

- Check your vehicle insurance covers you for Europe
- Ensure you have adequate European travel insurance cover
- While we're still in the European Union, apply for your free European Health Insurance Cards (EHIC). It's a five-minute job online at www.ehic.org.uk/Internet/startApplication.do
- Update your satnav with European mapping
- If you're travelling in France, by law you must disable the speed camera detectors on your satnav - the police will check

Sue & Rick loved touring Tuscany in their Paradise

- Loose change in the local currency for toll roads with unmanned booths
- GB stickers (unless your campervan has EU number plates, of course)

- Crit'Air stickers for some French cities - see *www.certificat-air.gouv.fr/en*
- Warning triangle (two for Spain)
- Reflective jackets - preferably one per person
- First aid kit
- Fire extinguisher
- Breathalyser kit (two per vehicle in France)
- Headlight deflectors - because you'll be driving on the right-hand side of the road
- Spare wheel
- Tyre inflator
- Spare car fuses and lamp bulbs
- European adaptor for filling up your campervan's LPG tank, if you have one
- Spare prescription glasses when driving in Switzerland
- Travel documents (originals) – passports, travel insurance
- Driving licence

- Campervan documents
- Membership cards and details for the Caravan and Motorhome Club
- ACSI Camping Card discount scheme
- Vehicle breakdown cover (AA, RAC), etc
- Maps (in case there's no signal for your satnav).
- An *All the Aires* book for the countries you plan to visit
- The France Passion Scheme guide
- Your ACSI card, if you've bought one

Handy to know

Some UK supermarkets, camping shops, and car accessory shops sell special European driving kits, which bundle together a number of the items listed above.

The law

Driving regulations vary from country to country. In some countries you have to be 18 years old to drive and in others it is 17. If in doubt, check the advice on the AA or RAC websites.

Dieppe diary - a last-minute family break to France

One of our favourite family breaks was our campervan trip around Normandy.

While there's plenty to see in the UK, holidays on the Continent mean a different culture, different food, and often different weather.

Day one: stocking & parking up

Upon arrival in Dieppe, we stock up on French food, so we can enjoy local dishes and delicacies from the start. It's fun loading up the fridge with delicious cheeses, meats, milk and the all-important ice-cream. With the larder full, we're ready to hit the coast.

On some holidays we do plan ahead - especially if there are specific places we want to visit and explore. But on this occasion we're keen to follow our noses and see where the road takes us.

We grab our *All the Aires* book and pick out Ault Onival in the Somme. When we arrive, there are lots of other motorhomes and campervans parked up, but we find a lovely sheltered spot away from the wind. After our first al-fresco French meal, we sit out and enjoy our first glass of wine on holiday, thinking – phew, we've made it!

Soon it's time for hot chocolate and our family bedtime story, which I read to everyone as we curl up in our sleeping bags. I normally get carried away only to find the children have fallen fast asleep... and then peace descends.

Day two: in the swim

It may be raining a little, but we're on holiday so nothing is stopping us from our morning visit to the boulangerie. After a mouthwatering breakfast we focus on our next destination. The boys say they want 'water slides and fun', so we're off to Domaine de Dancourt - only 30 minutes away.

Before arriving, we stock up at the local Carrefour supermarket (as campsite shops have less choice). We like cooking on our Cadac barbecue, so we choose tasty looking sausages and eggs for an easy tea, followed by delicious looking peaches. Even before we've booked in,

When travelling with a large family, we like to make the most of the outside space too the older boys are off into the swimming pool (it's one of the joys of camping - free range children).

After a good swim and a game of table tennis we head back to the campervan with all our wet towels. When it's a wet day, we use our indoor washing line in the roof. It is great. It is an essential accessory in every campervan, as we all have wet towels to dry.

Day three: history tour

The warm sun is shining... hurray! The boys are off so we get to relax for a good read in the sun. Bliss. Then it's off to visit St-Valery-Sur-Somme - a nearby medieval town famous as the location from which William the Conqueror set off with his fleet to attack England in 1066. It's a place full of interest and steeped in history.

It takes just a few minutes to get the campervan locked down and ready to go, and then we have the added luxury of our very own mobile café and private toilet. That's what I call travelling in style.

Day four: walking in sunshine

A good long walk in the French sunshine this morning does everyone good. It's one of the things we love about camping - the chance to enjoy plenty of fresh air and space. We always return home refreshed and relaxed.

There are beautiful wildflowers along the quiet roadside. The scenery makes me want to get an easel out and paint the tall poplar trees that are standing so handsomely along the path we have walked along.

Elijah is happy in the pushchair, especially when we see the donkeys. He is at the 'not quite walking' stage, and the campervan has room for him to move about without getting into trouble outside. This is handy, since he can move at quite a speed. It means we can sit down and enjoy a cup of tea together, without worrying constantly about what he is up to.

Why suffer the British winter, when you can enjoy a long break in Spain? Bobbie knows the best routes to the sun

Campervan owners often compare notes on the best ferry routes, so we asked VW Caledonia owner Bobbie for tips.

She says, "I escape to south of Spain during Britain's winter months, because, although there is some rain and it can be cold at night, most days are sunny and I can wear shorts all day, go to the beach, and sit outside to eat. The water is warm enough to swim in October and May but too cold for me from November to April. It doesn't stop my dog Willow from enjoying the sea most days. Food and drink is cheaper in Spain and I need less heating in my VW Caledonia than I would at home.

"I have travelled by four different routes from Calais to get to my favourite campsite in Altea, near Benidorm. In November most campsites are closed in France, so rather than stay at aires or service stations I use toll motorways; as a solo traveller, in the winter my aim is to reach my destination swiftly.

"In April, more French campsites are open, so to avoid tolls I drive a scenic route, through towns and villages and visit tourist attractions.

"Mostly I use Eurotunnel, and stay in the van with my dog and cat, but this year, I got the ferry from Portsmouth to Bilbao. A pet-friendly cabin meant my dog Willow and my cat Ebony were with me all the time. Then I drove to Zaragoza for one night, then on to Altea. My favourite route through France is the west coast: Rouen, Le Mans, Bordeaux, San Sebastian. I've also driven from Calais to Clermont Ferrand (avoiding Paris), then crossing the famous Millau Bridge.

"The campervan gives me the freedom to drive off and explore the area during my stay, without using public transport which does not allow dogs. Large motorhomes may have more space, but they don't allow such freedom. With a driveaway awning I can have plenty of room for long stays."

Bobbie heads south in her VW Caledonia every winter – and with views like that, who can blame her?

Bobbie has pet passports for her dog Willow and cat Ebony

Beyond Europe - new adventures.

"Next year I shall be going to Morocco after spending three months in Spain. I find that it is a much more rewarding experience if you can at least greet people, say goodbye, ask where something is, ask how much, and say please and thank you. It's very easy to get all these essential words on Google and write them down.

"There are also unspoken dress codes in different countries. For instance, I don't enter churches in beachwear. In remote places or Muslim countries, when I go out of the campsite I wear trousers or skirts below knee, and long sleeves. I research the customs of places and show respect by adopting the same manners. If you don't some locals may harass you, particularly if you are a lone female traveller.

"When buying things in shops, the prices are set, but in souks and markets, haggling is expected and can be fun. Stay friendly and smiling. Know your limit and stick to it. You can end up be very happy with the price, while they are still making a profit. They will run after you and lower the price, if you walk away, unless you have bid too low."

Chapter 7

Try something new

One of the joys of campervanning is that when you're out and about exploring a new place, you may get the urge to try something you've never done before

Stargazing

Light pollution means city dwellers rarely get to see the wonder in the sky after sunset. But with your campervan, you can try some amateur astronomy in comfort. Go to a Dark Skies Reserve, if you can. In the UK we have some of the darkest skies in the world. In fact, of the 11 International Dark Skies Reserves, four are British National Parks: the Brecon Beacons, Exmoor, Snowdonia and the South Downs. In addition, there are a number of Dark Sky Discovery Sites - you can find them on *www.darkskydiscovery.org.uk*

But what can you expect to see? Of course this will depend on the night sky, but as well as stars you can pick out constellations, the five brightest planets (Mercury, Venus, Mars, Jupiter and Saturn), and even the Milky Way. If you're lucky, you could also see some satellites and shooting stars.

Metal detecting

Another way to explore the great outdoors is through metal detecting. Armed with your trowel and metal detector and having obtained the landowner's permission, you can set off to find hidden 'treasure' (generally an item more than 300 years old and 10 percent gold or silver). It's a novel way to enjoy fresh air, with the excitement that you might discover something remarkable. And it's not a pipe dream. More than 90 per cent of treasures are discovered by amateurs with metal detectors, not professional archaeologists. If you do find treasure in England, you must report it to the local coroner within 14 days of finding it (see *www.gov.uk/treasure*).

Britain has a long history, so if you find a good hunting ground, you may well find long-forgotten metal objects. It's like stepping back in time.

Gazing at the heavens is more comfortable if you have a campervan

According to a recent BBC article, Norfolk is a treasure hotspot, with 116 treasure 'finds' a year, on average. Essex, Suffolk and Lincolnshire have also yielded more treasure than other parts of the country. You never know... your campervan might help you find a new hobby that you love.

Camp fire cooking

We find that there's something invigorating about being around a fire. There's the cracking wood, the smoky aroma, the warmth, and the dancing flames. A campfire extends an evening and offers the perfect focal point to bring everyone together.

Of course, camp fires aren't permitted everywhere you stay - so do check before striking the matches. But if a fire is possible, it's fun to make it a communal activity that involves everyone. Children will love collecting wood and toasting marshmallows.

Here's a quick guide to lighting the perfect fire.

You will need:

- Tinder (dry grass, small twigs, and dry leaves which light easily)
- Kindling (small sticks)
- Larger pieces of wood (to fuel the fire once it's started)

Make a small circle of tinder. Then, with your back to the wind, light the tinder with a match or lighter. As you add more tinder, gently blow at the base of the fire to help the flames catch. Once the tinder is well lit add some kindling, a little at a time. Then as the fire takes hold, add some of the larger pieces of fuel - remembering to ensure plenty of airflow.

Fire safety is common sense. Don't light the fire near anything that's flammable, especially your campervan or awning, a building or a tinder-dry forest floor in summer. Keep the size of the fire in check and under control and keep some water handy, just in case.

Finally, when you're done make sure you extinguish the fire completely. Cover with earth, sand or water and mix until there are no embers glowing.

Chris & Steph's spectacular campfire

What to cook

So, with your fire roaring away, what will you do with it? An old favourite is to toast marshmallows. Either use a metal fork with a plastic handle or a long spiky stick, and secure the marshmallow to the end. Dangle it over the fire (remembering to keep sleeves a safe distance from the flames) to cook. Turn frequently until the marshmallow begins to brown on the outside (and goes deliciously gooey on the inside). Then eat immediately, washed down with mugs of hot chocolate.

You could also try cooking jacket potatoes (sweet potatoes work well too). This can be a bit hit and miss, but for best results slice them in half first before wrapping them in tin foil (you can add butter between the two halves for extra flavour). Don't put the potatoes on top of the flames. Instead, place them in the embers. They'll take at least 45 minutes to cook - although sweet potatoes will be ready sooner. Try the same technique with foil wrapped bananas or peaches, but they only need ten minutes or so.

Let's go fly a kite - camping is family time

Flying a kite

There are lots of wide open, windy spaces in the UK that are perfect for kite flying. It's fun to experiment with tricks and twists.

Of course, you need to play safely. We tell our children to be aware of other people and watch out for dangers such as electricity pylons. They need to look behind them - so that they don't step over an edge.

It's good to start with a single line kite for just a few pounds. Then, if you get hooked, you can upgrade to an aerobatic sports kite.

Playing with nature

If you're campervanning with children and getting off the beaten track, then nature can become your playground. Here are our top suggestions for family fun.

Seaside fun

If you're near a beach you can try rockpooling. At some seaside locations you can go out with a guide, who will reveal the best places to look and identify the things you find. The tourist information people will advise. Go crabbing - it's a great way to spend a few hours soaking up the seaside atmosphere.

Foraging

Depending on the season, you could try picking wild garlic or blackberries. There's nothing more satisfying than eating food that you've collected yourself. If you've stocked up your campervan fridge-freezer you can eat the blackberries with ice-cream, yoghurt, or cream.

Building a den

Den building is an activity that kids of all ages love - and it's a great bonding experience. We like to hunt around for fallen branches and other natural materials and see what we can concoct.

Natural art

Take inspiration from the natural materials around you and create something beautiful, like bark and leaf rubbings, twig sculptures or painted pebbles.

Treasure trail

Lay a treasure hunt and challenge your children to find the things you've hidden in the trees. There's a current

On our beautiful island, you're never too far from the sea

craze for painting faces on pebbles and hiding them. If you find one, you hide it somewhere new.

Wildlife spotting

Try bird watching (and listening) and learn to mimic the calls - even better if you're visiting a place with where there's a hide.

- Identify the local trees from their leaves
- Spot flowers
- Look for wildlife
- Identify animal tracks and pretend to stalk them!
- Go on a minibeast hunt

Whittling

We let children have a go at whittling or wood carving - learning how to use tools carefully is a useful lesson.

When you unleash your imagination, it's remarkable what things you can enjoy - free of charge.

The National Trust also has an initiative called 50 Things To Do before You're 11¾. See www.nationaltrust.co.uk/50-things-to-do or pick up an activity book at a property. This list will keep children busy for a while and there are lots of things that you can tick off during your campervan adventures.

Cycling

When you have a campervan, it's easy to take your bikes with you. You can either throw them in the back or fit a bike rack to save space.

There are lots of beautiful cycle paths dotted all across the UK. Here's a small sample:

- The Camel Trail in Cornwall. Stretching from Wenford Bridge to Padstow, this 18-mile, virtually level trail takes you along the Camel estuary and its beautiful views. (www.cameltrailmap.co.uk).

- Lôn Mawddach Trail, North Wales. Stretching between Barmouth and Dolgellau, this 9.5-mile route (each way) follows a disused railway and offers stunning views of the Mawddach Estuary. (www.mawddachtrail.co.uk).

Richard's CamperCar takes him all over Europe

- The Cuckoo Trail in Sussex. This 14-mile railway track between Heathfield and Polegate is mostly traffic-free. With places to stop and relax, you can explore beautiful farmland and woodland as you cycle along.

- Taff Trail, South Wales. This 55-mile route is largely traffic-free and runs from Cardiff to Brecon. It's a great way to explore Cardiff and the surrounding area.

- Bealach na Bà, Scottish Highlands. This 43-mile circular route includes spectacular views across the the Isle of Skye and the Outer Hebrides.

An adrenalin activity

If you're an adrenalin junkie, then why not have a taste of an adventurous sport during your trip? Here are just a few ideas to whet your appetite:

Coasteering

This thrilling activity is an exciting way to enjoy a beautiful coastline. It combines cliff jumping with rock scrambling and even exploring sea caves (as well as swimming).

Gliding
Take to skies and enjoy a silent descent as you enjoy a bird's-eye-view.

Zip wires
A growing number of centres offer lengthy zipwire rides. Hold on tightly!

Kayaking or canoeing
Quiet paddling in a small boat means you can get closer to any sea life. If you fancy something a little more daring, there are many rivers across the UK where you can brave the rapids and thrills of white water.

High ropes
Climb up to treetop level and and navigate obstacles suspended high above the ground in family activity centres such as Go Ape. Depending on the course, you can try swinging, climbing and even free-falling.

A campervan is the perfect place to dry off after water sports

David has been exploring the UK in his campervan and is looking to branch out into Europe soon

"I stayed near Bala Lake in Wales last summer on my first major trip in the campervan. I thought the two kayaks would prove to be a drag on performance, but this was not the case. I've also been down to Exeter and Bristol and up to Norfolk to see the seals pupping in December.

"I have to say that the van has been everything I had wished for. I have no regrets about the layout that I chose. I will be taking it to Spain or Italy next summer, so I'm looking forward to that."

Dedicated runners Tim and his wife Karen have just bought a Nissan NV200 CamperCar with an automatic gearbox

Tim says, "We'll be using the camper as a base vehicle for running, and as a great place to change and stay dry when it's raining.

"Karen is the best runner. She's from Wales, and we've moved from Hailsham in Sussex to Cumbria, where I grew up. I'm looking forward to using the campervan to show her the Lake District."

Michael found a 1,000-year-old Anglo-Saxon penny during one trip in his Nissan CamperCar

"As a keen treasure hunter and landscape photographer, my campervan enables me to spend more time enjoying the hobbies I love. I'm out detecting every weekend and I often go away for rallies or trips with my local club. It's a fun hobby. In fact, I often say it's like Christmas, because you never know what you're going to turn up next.

"The oldest thing I've found dates from between 1500-2000 BC. It was a Bronze Age artefact. I've found bells that animals wore around their neck, and a beehive

thimble from the 14th century. I've discovered lots of coins, including 2,000-year-old Roman coins, silver coins from the time of Elizabeth I and James I, as well as coins bearing the head of Charles II. I'm always curious to discover the history behind my finds, so I find myself learning a lot about history, without even trying.

"I had my best find to date just before Christmas 2015, when I discovered an Anglo-Saxon penny bearing Edward The Confessor's head. This coin was dated from around 1056 (10 years before the Battle of Hastings). The name of the coin maker was on the back: Africk. I've since discovered that he was one of the last Anglo Saxon moneyers before the Norman Conquest.

"The campervan - which I just call Nissie - is my daily drive and it provides me a base for my detecting activities and a nice warm and dry place for lunch. The table serve provides a work space to record finds at lunchtime, found by club members. I hope that, this year

I will have more in the way of finds and some longer weekend outings with friends.

"I bought a campervan because it was the right choice for my hobbies and my lifestyle. When it was time to buy a new car, I wanted something more versatile and flexible. I didn't want two cars, so I bought an NV200 CamperCar to double up as an everyday vehicle. It's economical and easy to drive.

"My CamperCar has made things so much easier. Now I can travel that little bit further afield. Or if I'm out for the day, I have somewhere to relax with a hot cup of tea. It's great to be able to sit around a proper table and have a chat with friends!"

Michael takes his NV200 CamperCar metal detecting in Wiltshire

Chapter 8

Maximum campervan storage

How to pack your campervan for convenience and luxury

Packing is so important when you own a campervan. We are often asked: "Can you really get all you need for a holiday into one vehicle?" Many people assume that they'll find it restrictive because the camper is 'small', but a campervan with a well designed interior is deceptively spacious. You don't need suitcases; the camper itself is like a big wardrobe.

That said, we've found we need to travel light. Forget all the trappings of your house, and start with the essentials. That's one of the joys of campervanning: minimalism and living a simpler life while you're away from it all.

Comfort isn't the only reason to pack wisely. Every ounce you can leave at home will boost your fuel efficiency. So, we take items that have a multi-purpose if possible.

We like to stock up with food as we go and use launderettes and campsite facilities to wash and dry things when we need to, rather than take loads of clothing with us.

Being organised

The secret to a feeling of spaciousness in your camper is to put items away after use. We visualise how we'll use the campervan when deciding where to put everything. We put complementary items close to each other.

Adding extra storage

The beauty of ordering a 'built to order' bespoke modern van conversion is that the interior of your vehicle can be designed around you. We suggest you base your choices on one of the tried and tested layouts that maximise space and storage, then ask your campervan converter how you can accommodate any particular items that you want to take with you.

There are other ways to add storage after you've bought your campervan:

- Back seat car tidies/organisers are brilliant for tablets and hairbrushes.
- We've bought a box that just fits neatly under the back of the Rock 'n' Roll bed, for walking boots, waterproofs and a portable barbecue.
- It's worth asking your van converter if they can add roof rails to the pop-top roof, so you can take lightweight things in a roof box.
- Many people add a bike rack.
- We take collapsible silicone buckets for wet things.
- We store bulky items - such as folding chairs - under the vehicle when we're parked up.

Here's our essential campervan packing checklist:

Kitchen
- Kettle, two nesting saucepans, frying pan, cutlery, melamine plates, bowls and mugs, wooden utensils, BBQ tongs, kitchen roll, tea towel, towel

- Food basics: pasta, pasta sauce, bread, butter, milk, spreads, breakfast cereal, salt, pepper, ketchup, cooking oil, bacon and eggs
- Washing up liquid, brush, scourer and a bowl (to take to the campsite kitchen)

Toiletries
- Toilet rolls: the quick dissolving type for cassette toilets to prevent clogging up the exit pipe
- Baby wipes: these have multiple cleaning uses for you and your camper
- Toothpaste and toothbrush
- Shower gel
- Sponge/flannel
- Shampoo and conditioner
- Liquid soap
- A wash bag
- Towels: thin, lightweight ones or even micro fibre towels that dry super-fast
- Sun cream and after sun

- Hand sanitiser

Pack your clothes

- Pack your campervan lockers directly, as if you were using cupboards at home
- Take clothes that are quick to wash and dry
- Pack underwear for a week
- Choose clothes that go together in different ways to maximise your choice of outfits
- Layer up – for comfort, whatever the weather
- Remember swimming gear and beach towels
- Take warm socks, blankets and layers for evening barbecues

Sleeping

Sleeping bag or sheets and duvets: the choice is yours. Compression storage bags are handy. Take pillows and use them as sofa cushions by day.

Fleece blankets are lightweight, easy to wash and dry, and warm on cold nights.

Jacky's duvet matches our Sussex Campervans stag

Personal items

- Mobile phone and charger
- Something to read
- Notebook and pens
- Camera and batteries

Entertainment

- Pack of cards and board games
- Books and magazines
- A box of 'stuff' for the kids
- Puzzle books
- Bucket and spade (if you're off to the beach)
- Music
- A ball

Camping essentials

- Plastic bags for rubbish, wet clothes
- A dustpan and brush
- Torch and spare batteries
- Washing-up liquid (Ecover is good for wild camping)
- Laundry powder
- Citronella candles to keep insects away at night
- Portable washing line and pegs
- First aid kit
- Camping chairs and table
- Kitchen spray cleaner
- Dishcloth/sponge
- Gas
- Portable barbecue - either gas or charcoal with firelighters
- Lighter
- Groundsheet: for the awning and the beach
- Small rucksack for picnic walks and beach days

These essentials cover the basics, but everyone has their own comforts that they can't do without. I suggest a brainstorming session, to list down all of yours.

With our growing family, we face a holiday packing challenge...

We hadn't got around to organising a holiday, but that didn't matter. With our family campervan ready and waiting, we knew that we could take a last-minute holiday to France. Decision made, two days later we drove to Newhaven, for the lovely four-hour Channel crossing to Dieppe.

We picked that ferry route because we wanted to explore the Normandy coastline, without driving too far. Newhaven is a small port, so that usually means quick and easy boarding.

We have a big family. With seven children and two adults, that's nine in total. When we all go away we have no choice but to use a big motorhome, but on this occasion - with some of the older children opting to stay at home - we travelled as a six. Our 'Manhattan MPV' campervan was the perfect size.

Careful packing was in order. Fortunately, our van conversion has lots of tidy storage places and plenty of room to store everything that a large family needs for a memorable summer break.

Our 'wardrobe' has been customised with three shelves, so our older boys can have a shelf each. The shelves are a good size so they can put away all their shorts and T-shirts and still reach them in the morning.

Ottoman bed for the youngest

Our youngest was just one at the time of this trip, so not only did he need more 'stuff' than the rest of us put together, he needed somewhere safe to sleep.

We quickly found a solution. With the help of our workshop, we created a guard that flipped up at night on the ottoman. This worked really well. My smallest son was close to me and I knew he wouldn't roll out of bed at night, or get frightened.

Everything fits in cupboards for travel, and there's plenty of room to spread out when we're parked

Even when travelling with six, Rebekah has a place for everything in our campervan

Room for everyone and everything

I used the spacious cupboard below the hob to store all the kitchen utensils and food.

The under-bed cupboard is big. We used it to stow a two-man tent (in case the boys wanted to camp), the waterproofs for everyone, and baby Elijah's clothes. I also left room for anything we might bring home from our holidays, such as French wine.

The under-bed cupboard was also ideal for items you won't need in the middle of the night (such as towels), as well as a laundry bag for dirty clothes .

The cupboard under the ottoman was used to store shoes, UHT milk, toilet rolls, nappies, swimming costumes, an inflatable crocodile, the baby swimming seat, and other bits and bobs.

In the boot we had our folding picnic table, two folding chairs, a large groundsheet to stop mud coming in to the campervan, a Cadac portable camping stove (we love to do most of our big cooking outside in the sunshine), a bag with the electric hook-up cables, the children's spades, badminton racquets, frisbee, and table tennis bats tucked in at the side and a football.

Safety kit is a 'must'

Under the cab seats we packed: a first aid kit, two hi-vis jackets and a warning triangle, plus the silver screens to go round the cab windows for extra insulation. I also have a folding canvas box for all our books on the floor in the cab.

In the pop-top roof we store flattened out sleeping bags on top of the roof boards, for the older boys. We put our own sleeping bags folded up on the back seat and two small sleeping bags and pillows went in the storage area under the ottoman.

Catherine and Dan are both teachers, and they enjoy all-weather holidays with their two children

"As a family we've always been into camping. Until recently we had a tent, but I've always fancied a campervan. So, after a family event left us some money, we decided to introduce our two children to the joys of the road.

"With two children, we knew we'd need a fair bit of storage space, so we bought a long-wheel-based Renault Trafic van with a bespoke interior. It's ideal.

"Having the freedom to customise the interior to suit our needs was a real bonus. Instead of a cupboard, we ordered a large ottoman. This gave us huge storage capacity and is perfect for storing all the bits and bobs we need when we're away. In fact, there's enough room for a three-week holiday. We pack a week's worth of clothes and then use the campsite's on-site laundrette when we need clean ones. And everything is kept neat, tidy, and accessible with the help of storage boxes and our fabulous ottoman.

"We've been away a lot. The kids just love it and even though we've had our van for four years now, the novelty hasn't worn off. They love sleeping in the pop up roof - and showing off the campervan to their friends.

"The camper is deceptively spacious. Sometimes it's nice to have some adult-only space, but we've got the awning for that. It makes a nice, spacious, outside lounge/dining area, and somewhere for the kids to play.

"The campervan has extended our camping season. One year we camped in December so we could attend a Christmas market. As the van is so well insulated, it's really cosy in colder weather.

"As we're teachers, we're able to make the most of the school holidays to get away. We always go away for three weeks in the summer and we enjoy day trips, weekends, and mini breaks during the year. For example, we've been to Sussex and the Cotswolds and we're going to the Yorkshire Dales and the North Yorkshire coast this summer.

"We had a lovely trip in France visiting the Dordogne and Brittany, and another year we went to Austria. That was amazing. The scenery was breathtaking and it was great for cycling (which we all love).

"With our bike rack it's so easy to take bikes for the whole family. The campsites were fantastic and everything was so family friendly. At one place there was a lake where you could go swimming or boating - and there were cafés and restaurants around the water. It was so beautiful and relaxing.

"We find travelling is easier in the campervan. While the kids do argue over who sits next to the big window, we've solved that problem with a strict rota! The kids love it because there's space on their seats for their stuff and the tinted windows keep the sun out of their eyes.

"We love our campervan. We love the flexibility and freedom of being able to park up somewhere for the night before we head off again. This has opened up lots more opportunities for discovering new places. With the tent, we'd only consider camping for a minimum of a week. Any shorter was just too much hassle.

"We have lots more day trips. It's really handy having somewhere dry to sit after a muddy walk. A cup of tea brewed in your own campervan tastes delicious.

"We look forward to creating lots more happy family memories in the months and years ahead."

Catherine & Dan enjoy going abroad with their family

Chapter 9

Micro living: how to love life on 4 wheels

Take the fast track to campervan living with our tips...

While you might love the idea of campervan freedom, you may still be wary about how you'll survive on the road. So what can you do to ensure the campervan lifestyle exceeds your expectations and becomes something you love?

Fortunately, there are lots of simple things you can do to make the experience fun and carefree.

Cleaning

With a much smaller space to look after, your campervan is easier to clean than your house. In fact, you could say that 'housework' is a doddle! The secret is to stay on top of it. When you've used any crockery, wash it and put it away. Don't leave things lying around; clutter and mess can hamper your enjoyment.

Keep a dustpan and brush handy so you can sweep the floor regularly. Use slippers or flip-flops to keep the worse of the dust and mud outside.

Washing your clothes

Clothes washing is so easy at home, thanks to modern appliances. Fortunately, good campsites have laundry facilities, too, which means you can cut down on your packing and continue to wear your favourite clothes on holiday.

We take a laundry bag, so we can keep dirty clothes in one place, plus portable washing line and pegs. In hotter climes, wet clothes dry in a flash, and you can hang up swimwear and towels after a day at the beach.

Washing clothes can become a game for families; if you hand wash a few clothes in the washing-up bowl your little ones can join in. Just give them small items like socks. And when it's hot, who cares if you end up having a water fight? We've had our fair share over the years.

Routine

This is especially useful if you have children, or more than two people in the van.

First thing in the morning and bedtimes are often the hotspots - when you switch your camper from night to day mode (and vice versa). Children can be bouncy and excitable when they first wake up. So, we give them a quick snack and a drink and let them play in the awning while we get everything set up for meal times. If you don't have an awning, children can play in the pop-up roof, in the front seats or outside (if it's safe). Explaining to children very clearly what you want them to do - and why - helps, of course.

Teamwork is often the way to ensure everyone is happy and having fun. When you're on holiday there are always little jobs that need doing. So, why not allocate tasks and get everyone involved? By making children responsible for these small jobs, you can teach them how to tackle new life skills.

Consider:

- Sharing out the jobs and working as a team - it's a lot more fun and things happen far quicker and easier if each child knows what tasks are considered their responsibility.

- Allocating morning chores. The first person who wakes up puts the kettle on while the other person puts the bed back into day mode.
- A rule that the kids must stay outside when it's time to cook (weather permitting).
- Letting the children wash up, while you have a quiet cuppa. There's no hurry - it's fine if the children take an hour to wash a few plates. So what - they did it. Most campsites have very clean washing-up facilities and plenty of hot water.

Experiment and see what works for you, but the name of the game is to find ways to ensure life runs as smoothly as possible.

Hygiene

How do you go about washing and (erm) 'toileting' in your campervan? I'm glad you asked. Let's talk about the toilet first.

Most conversions will have an on-board toilet, which sits discreetly in a cupboard until it's needed. This means if you'd rather not use public (or campsite) amenities, you

Sue's washing dried quickly among the olive trees in this laid back Italian campsite

Chris & Gemma took their children for a picnic at the beach for their first trip

won't have to. And there's no nipping out in the night with a torch...

Dosing the chemical WC with the right product eliminates odour. You won't even know there's a toilet on board. When the toilet is full, you simply empty the contents of the removable cassette into a waste disposal point (available on all campsites), and that's it. A public WC can make do as well.

You can also wash in the campervan sink. Simply heat up some water and have a strip wash in the privacy of your vehicle. It is possible to have a very comfortable stay - even if there are limited facilities where you choose to park overnight.

If you're staying on a campsite, clean hot showers and plenty of flushing toilets are available. It's almost as good as being at home - well, better, because they do all the cleaning!

Your campervan should have plug sockets, so as long as you're hooked up to electricity you can use appliances such as hairdryers and straighteners. And if you want to have a shave or put on make-up, you can hang a mirror in your campervan or have one discreetly inside a cupboard door.

Privacy

You may think that in a small space you won't have privacy, but your campervan can be designed to maximise space for privacy - if that's important to you.

The classic side kitchen layout is very popular. It creates plenty of space to move around when the seats are in day mode and there is more sleeping capacity with this interior. However, there isn't a specific area you can cordon off.

In our Paradise conversions, that can be resolved by the galley kitchen, located in the rear of the vehicle. A divider or a curtain can create two distinct zones. With this layout you can use the toilet in private, have breakfast in bed, and enjoy full access to the kitchen - day and night.

You can also create extra space and privacy by putting up a drive-away awning. Many people use the 'porch' part of it for the portable toilet at night.

Securely fastened to the side of your vehicle, a drive-away awning is an extra room. If you need a few minutes alone inside your campervan, everyone else can move to the awning. And once you've put up your picnic tables and chairs, your awning will become a lovely space to relax.

Parking up

One of the best things about travelling in your campervan is that the outdoors becomes an extension of your home. Of course, you'll want to position your vehicle to make best use of the views (ensuring you're nice and level if you're planning to stay the night).

Children love to get off the beaten track and explore their new surroundings, but you'll want them to do that safely, where you can keep an eye on them.

Jacky and Michael use their awning for extra storage

Temperature

It is possible to use your campervan in all seasons and all weathers. With the heater going, you'll soon get your vehicle toasty warm. And of course with the gas hob, you can prepare warming meals and hot drinks. Simply throw in some extra warm clothes, your favourite sleeping bag, and perhaps a fleece blanket or two and the frost won't bite on a cold winter's night.

You'll also want to keep your camper cool on those hot summer nights, by opening the mesh vents in your pop-top tent. There are plenty of electric fans that plug into your 12V sockets. And for the simple option, park up with your door in the shade, as that allows some cooler air to circulate. Remember, you can make good use of your fridge-freezer too. From cold drinks, to ice cubes, and ice-cream, simply top up with treats to cool you down.

Rain shouldn't stop the fun

When it comes to camping, you have no influence over the weather and there's always the chance your trip will be interrupted by rain. But here's the good thing...

unlike a tent you have a much better chance of keeping things dry.

So here are some of our top tips for surviving rubbish weather and ensuring it doesn't ruin your holiday:

Use a drive-away awning

An awning creates a sheltered space outside your campervan and allows you to open your door without fear of the rain getting inside. The fresh air will do everyone good and if the rain is lighter, you could even sit outside and stay dry. An awning is a also handy place to keep stuff dry or hang up wet clothing.

Prevent things from getting wet

If it looks like rain, try to bring things inside before they get too wet.

Make a 'no shoes indoors' rule

Rain makes the ground muddy, and if you're not careful your campervan can soon become dirty. A clean campervan is a delight, so we have indoor shoes or flip-flops for everyone. That way, welly boots and muddy shoes can be left outside – preferably turned upside-down, tucked under the campervan, or covered up, so they don't get wet inside.

Use plastic bags

If you've been caught in the rain then you may return to your campervan soaked. We tend to pop all the wet gear into a plastic carrier bag and place it out of the way in the front foot-wells of the van. Then we can wash and dry these items later.

Stay warm

Whether it means putting on a brew, getting cosy under a fleecy blanket, or switching on the heater, it's worth trying to stay toasty warm.

Enjoy quality time together

If you've packed wet weather activities, just in case, then you can watch something on your iPad, listen to music, read, draw, do a puzzle, grab a pack of cards, or play a game. It's fun spending that time together and with a little luck those rain clouds will blow away, having refreshed the plants.

Wet weather is a chance to cook...

If it's wet outside, we sometimes prepare something a little more adventurous for dinner. It's easy to while away a few hours sipping a glass of something while you prepare a tasty meal for everyone. Or, if all else fails, we pop on the kettle and eat cake. Yum!

Take a drive

A downpour may make it more difficult to enjoy the scenery, but we never know where we might end up.

Plan tomorrow's trip

Grabbing the map, or guidebooks or searching the internet, we all decide what to see next.

Pack up and drive to the sunshine

With a campervan you're never tied to a specific location. It can pay to grab a phone, check out the forecast elsewhere and head for better weather.

Why wait for retirement to have fun? Nicola uses her camper for both the commute to work and leisure time

Working as a peripatetic NHS clinician means that Nicola spends a lot of time driving to hospitals around Kent and Sussex. On her travels she'd noticed quite a few professionals using campervans as mobile offices and a place to bed down, and it got her thinking. Could she buy a campervan to use for both work and pleasure?

Nicola has named her CamperCar 'Ophelia'

She certainly didn't fancy driving a great big motorhome around every day, but was there something more car-like that she could buy? Storm Ophelia was about to break, but in the half-light a gleaming silver Nissan NV200 CamperCar caught Nicola's eye, and after taking it for a drive, she decided that was exactly the right size for what she needed.

She says, "I am so glad I didn't wait until I retired to join the campervan gang. Life is for living... not waiting, and it is definitely for sharing and giving, which I can do more of now with my fabulous new wheels."

Like so many campervan owners, she has given her van a name. She says, "Ophelia is really beautifully crafted and lovely to drive. We will be going to work every day round Kent and camping out to cut down my work miles. Then it's back to Sussex at weekends and up to Scotland for holidays."

Angela and Trevor, from Saffron Walden, received their campervan in February and couldn't wait to use it

Angela said, "We took our grandson with us on our first trip in the Nissan NV200 CamperCar in February. He loved it. We did have two lovely sunny days and it was so good on the beach. We searched the shoreline for treasure and spent hours skimming stones.

"For our second winter camping trip we chose the North Norfolk coast. The wind was bitter, but the days were full of sunshine and blue skies, so we did a lovely walk to Brancaster on the coast path. The CamperCar heater made it bearable at night and our dog, Bonnie, lay on us like a hot water bottle. We thought, if we can camp in this Siberian weather, it will be amazing in the summer.

"In May we went on a 19-day tour of Scotland. We are fans of the TV drama Outlander, so we based our holiday on visiting the film locations, and beyond." After 15 days touring most of Scotland, they camped beside Loch Lomond. "We didn't move we stayed sunbathing by Loch all day, it was beautiful... our first day of not doing anything! We love the camper. Lots of people stopped to speak to us and admired the camper's size and what we had in there. We did 1800 miles and loved every minute of it. We're planning more trips, including Route 500 up to John o'Groats and down to Oban."

Angela and Trevor camped by Loch Lomond

John and Gail are having so much fun, they blame their campervan for the fact they're never at home

John & Gail stayed near the Thames on one trip

John says, "Since we bought our fabulous campervan we have not been home much. It's just so easy. We load up and away we go. If it's not trips to see our grandchildren (one lot in the north and the others on the south coast), we'll see what takes our fancy and go where we want to, both here in the UK or abroad.

"We recently went to the F1 Grand Prix in Monza, Italy. Gail pointed out that we weren't too far from Venice, so we jumped back in the van, headed to the 'City of Love' and had a wonderful time there.

"We spent a lot of time in London at the Queen's birthday celebrations, after getting tickets to her party in Windsor Castle, and we've just returned from three weeks in France. We have a Vivaro-based van conversion, which is super. It travels really well on the autoroutes and motorways. We get lots of admiring looks when we are travelling. What on earth did we do before we had our campervan?"

Chapter 10

Campervan cuisine

How we cook delicious food on two hobs

One of the big attractions for many people when they're considering buying a campervan is the ability to stop when you fancy and eat where and when you choose. This life is all about freedom.

Most campervans have a two-ring gas hob, which is enough for preparing delicious and varied meals. So rest assured... you're not restricted to pasta, a sandwich, and a cup of tea.

In addition, you can always take a portable BBQ if you want to cook outside. With convenient self-catering, you don't have to spend a fortune on eating out, which means your holiday budget can stretch quite a lot further, and you can eat better, healthier food.

Cooking in a campervan rarely feels like hard work. If you buy good ingredients and cook them simply, they will taste even better in the campervan than they do at home. Perhaps it's the fresh air, the adventure, or the fact that you're relaxed. Maybe it's all three!

And because you're self-catering, you can also make the most of local farm shops, markets, and roadside stalls. These are the perfect places to stock up on fresh local specialities, free-range eggs, local meats and cheese and artisan breads for a scrumptious al fresco dining experience, in tune with the area you're visiting.

You may find yourself near a pick-your-own farm. If so, it's worth gathering whatever is in season and using the ingredients in your next meal.

So, while you may want to treat yourself to the occasional evening out, once you've found an idyllic spot or campsite, nothing tastes better than some home cooked food with a view of the sunset. My personal favourite is fresh Tagliatelle...

Space for food preparation

We use our campervan table to get everything ready. From chopping veggies to preparing a salad there's enough room to prepare for a family feast.

Manhattan owners Bill & Elsa enjoy eating al-fresco and sampling local food and wines

Cook's checklist

After many years of campervanning with a family, we've got our kitchen packing list down to a 'T'.

Here's what we recommend:

- Tea bags, coffee, herbal teas, and hot chocolate powder in airtight containers
- Cafetière and freshly ground coffee
- Biscuits in an airtight container
- A box of unopened cereal
- Kids love the novelty of individual variety packs of cereal
- UHT milk for emergencies
- Pasta and a jar of pasta sauce
- Rice and couscous
- Spreads: Marmite, Nutella, jam, honey, marmalade, peanut butter
- Cooking oil

There's plenty of extra storage in the Paradise Twin

- Seasonings: salt, pepper, tomato ketchup, instant gravy powder, herbs and spices

Kitchen essentials

Look for space savers: things that stack or fold and items with a multi-purpose.

- An aluminium, lightweight whistling kettle
- Two nesting aluminium saucepans with lids - small and large - or swap the big pan for a deep sauté pan or a griddle
- A steamer - boil potatoes in the pan below and green vegetables above
- Chopping board
- Sharp knife
- Scissors
- Potato peeler
- Tin opener
- A flat cheese grater
- Wooden spoon
- Wooden spatula
- Serving spoon
- Large bowl for salads and pasta
- Bottle opener and corkscrew
- A tray
- Cutlery: knife, fork, spoon, and teaspoon per person
- Melamine crockery - it's lightweight, scratch-resistant and less breakable, but don't put it in the microwave, if you have one
- Kitchen towel
- Measuring cups and spoons

Two hobs not enough?

It's possible to do loads with two hobs and basic utensils, but you can add more equipment when you're hooked up to the mains on a campsite.

Microwave ovens

Some vans do have a built-in microwave, but if yours doesn't you could buy a small one to take with you. It's handy if you want to heat up a quick meal, cook jacket potatoes, or make hot chocolate before bed.

Slow cookers

If we're staying on a campsite, we sometimes pop meat and a sauce in a slow cooker and leave it to cook while we're out enjoying the day on bikes or on foot. By the time we come back, it smells delicious and is ready to serve up, with bread, pasta or rice.

Barbecues

Barbecues make cooking outside a breeze. If you don't want to 'faff' with charcoal, consider a compact portable Cadac. We attach ours to the gas bottle (or external BBQ point) in the campervan and use it to cook everything from a fried breakfast to a roast chicken. These meals are absolutely delicious to eat outdoors.

Easy washing up

After the joy of cooking comes the lovely job of the washing up. Most people load it all into a collapsible plastic crate and use the campsite kitchen facilities. Alternatively, we put the kettle on while we eat so we can wash things in the campervan sink afterwards.

- We think carefully about which utensils, crockery, and cutlery we use, trying to avoid making unnecessary mess. Where possible, we prepare one-pot or two-pan meals and reuse pans for more than one thing. If meals take longer to wash up than to prepare, have a rethink

- We like non-stick pans that are easy to wash

- We wipe everything with kitchen towel before washing up, to save hot water

- It's best to wash the cleanest dishes first and save the greasiest for last

- Rinsing everything separately can help - we do this by popping a bowl onto the table

- We allow the dishes to drain on a tray covered with a towel. This cuts the number of tea towels needed

- We put things away only when they're dry, to prevent damp getting inside the cupboards

Disposing of the dishwater wisely is easy on a campsite as there will be designated areas. But if you're wild camping, do be sensitive and consider the environment.

Once the hob has cooled, you can put the glass lids down for some extra workspace

Nick, Georgie and son Harry love eating in their camper

Georgie says, "I'm enjoying exploring different menus and dishes in our camper's kitchen. It's amazing what you can rustle up on the hob!" Here is one of her favourite camping weekend meal plans.

Friday evening
Fried salmon with a wedge of lime, a ready seasoned pack of couscous, a tin of chickpeas, salad and a crème fraîche and garlic dip.

Saturday breakfast
Bacon and egg banjos, with black pudding for me (I hate bacon).

Saturday lunch
Chicken and watercress paninis - lightly toasted, with a bit of garlic butter, with a choice of mango chutney or mayo in the sandwich (or both).

Saturday evening
Sausage and red pesto pasta with salad.

Sunday breakfast
Cereal, if we are packing up.

Sunday lunch
Stopping on the way home and quickly making cheese on toast, or Harry's new favourite: Quesadillas.

Campervan puddings
Yoghurts, fruits or ice creams - from our lovely little campervan freezer box.

Georgie loves cooking family meals on the go

Chapter 11

Family first: making memories to last a lifetime

When did you first fall in love with campervans?

Lettie told us:

"I was between 5 and 10. We lived in a small village and a relative came to visit in a campervan, he was a 'Beatnik'. It seemed quite exotic. There were fewer cars around then, in the early 1960s. My dear Dad was probably still driving a Ford Popular then!"

For Ian, the passion began at birth. He says:

"I was driven home from the hospital in a Splittie after being born... so I think I fell in love with campervans pretty early on!"

As parents, if we ever enjoyed family camping holidays as children, we know that the outdoor life is something wonderful we can pass on to our own children, helping them to become more resourceful and adaptable.

Childhood seems to go way too quickly. As each busy school year rolls into the next, soon we find ourselves looking back at pictures of little ones in our arms, wondering where those years went.

Growing up (and away) is inevitable, and that's why memories of our children are so important, both for us and for them.

Owning a campervan can help to create priceless memories of moments, adventures, and conversations that we've enjoyed together. If the weather is good, we can get away for the weekend, any time of the year.

Why do children love camping?

Kids love the freedom and adventure of being outside. They soon get restless if they're cooped up for too long. It's one of the big draws of camping holidays. In a hotel we'd have to keep our kids quiet for the sake of the other guests; on campsites there are usually children's play areas, where they can run free and make new friends.

Family day trips are a breeze, because we have more room when travelling, as well as somewhere warm, dry, and cosy to use as a base when we're out.

Tips for stress-free adventures

Here are some things that have kept our children happy on journeys:

Little treats handy for a snack

We leave packets of crisps on the worktop and store heavier items in a cupboard that's easy to reach while we're journeying along.

Entertainment items

In many campers, you can leave the table up in the back and provide a box of games, toys, and colouring books to keep them busy. Our children like sticker books, Playmobil and cards. You could also consider installing 'back of the seat' portable DVD players or take tablets and smartphones with you. Seat tidies can help you maximise space too.

A chance to bagsie the front seat

For a change of scenery, we let the older children take turns to sit up front with the driver. This is a great way to spend one-to-one time with each child. They value the quality time and also enjoy seeing the road from the lofty perspective of the front seat.

Taking breaks

The journey itself becomes part of the holiday, so it's easy to weave in stops. Short bursts of travel suit our children, because they hate sitting still for long stretches of time.

Avoiding the motorway

When we're travelling abroad, we'll often avoid the motorways. We'll simply look at the map to see what looks interesting and plan our route around key highlights. Off the motorway, not only is it easier to stop, but we can enjoy better scenery and a glimpse of local life. We've found that a scenic detour doesn't add too much time to journeys in Europe, though they add hours to your travelling time in Britain.

Drive before breakfast

If we have a long journey ahead, we'll clock up a couple of hours before breakfast. This is one of the advantages of having a campervan rather than a tent or a caravan -

Our son Elijah loves to be in the driving seat

you can be away in minutes. Simply put the vehicle into day mode, lock down the roof, unplug, turn on the ignition and you're off. We let the kids stay in their pyjamas, give them a quick snack and head off to a nice spot for breakfast.

After everyone is nice and full, we'll head off again and find somewhere for a long lunch... preferably somewhere the kids can play and we can relax. We'll finish the journey after lunch and by the time we've arrived at our destination, we feel as though we've spent a day on holiday.

Places to stay

Children can be fairly easy to please. They love the novelty of sleeping and travelling in the campervan and younger children will relish the chance to spend more time with mum and dad.

Our children also love the freedom and adventure that typifies a campervan holiday. The chance to be outside and make new friends means they'll get up to all sorts of adventures that don't necessarily need to involve us - so we can enjoy quality parent-only time too. Then we can sit outside the campervan with a glass of something at sunset. We don't need to feel cooped up when the youngest kids have gone to bed.

Things to do

When we choose to stay on a family campsite with all the amenities, our children are never bored. Plenty of commercial sites offer swimming pools, flumes, play parks and even kids' clubs with free activities to keep little ones busy.

Alternatively, we:

- Go for a walk, take a picnic, and see what we find
- Take our bikes and head off on a trail
- Go to the beach
- Explore the woods, climb some trees, and spot animal tracks, birds and plants
- Spend the day by the river in the great outdoors
- Go to a theme park
- Visit a National Trust or English Heritage property
- Try a new sport - anyone for tennis?

Matthew loved the playground at this family campsite

Jeremy, his wife Janice, their son Julian, and their dog Pebbles use their campervan 'Laurence' for windsurfing and other adventures in the great outdoors

Jeremy says, "As a family, we love being outdoors. We always used to go camping, but began getting fed up with being cold and wet in a tent, so we decided to explore several other options.

"We didn't want a caravan, because of the hassle of storage and towing, and I know how long it can take to get a caravan ready to go. That was one of the things that attracted us to a campervan - we knew we could leave it packed, and go when we like. So we decided to swap our car for a campervan.

"We get away in it just about every weekend. It's such a big part of our life, that I wouldn't go back to buying a car again. I'd even say that the camper is easier to drive, because the wing mirrors are so much bigger - you get a much better view of the road.

"Laurence suits our lifestyle perfectly. We love hiking, mountain biking, and windsurfing, so it's great to have the space to chuck everything we need into the back and just head off. We carry windsurfing boards on a rack on the roof.

Jeremy & Janice swapped their car for a camper

"The campervan is compact and easy to park just about anywhere. We don't need a plan and, while we hope the weather is good, it really doesn't matter. The van is so cosy that the rain needn't spoil our fun. If we want to create more room we just pop up our awning. Simple.

"Owning a campervan has made our family stronger. Our son is 15, but still finds camping with us exciting. He sees it as an adventure and is a willing participant. I'm grateful for this. It's not unusual for teenagers to want to go off and do their own thing, so we're happy that he still wants to come away with us in the campervan.

"The van comfortably sleeps the three of us, and sometimes our son will bring a friend along. And even if he doesn't, there are always other teenagers at the campsite who he can hang out with when he gets bored with us."

When we first spoke to Jeremy they had only had the campervan a few months, but already they'd enjoyed lots of adventures and made plenty more plans. They were going to Scotland and the Isle of Mull for two weeks in the summer and had only planned a couple of night stops. After that, they decided to follow their

"I only wish I'd done this sooner" says Jeremy

noses. Jeremy says, "It's one of the best things about owning a campervan - the freedom and the flexibility. If we want to extend our stay somewhere we can. And if we want to move on, we can do that too.

"Buying a campervan for our family was a brilliant decision. I only wish I'd done it when Julian was a lot younger. Saying that, we are certainly making up for lost time now."

Those who experience campervan life as children will never lose their appetite for adventure, says Kieron

"As a child I used to camp with my family. I've got fond memories of things I did with my parents and I wanted my children to have similar experiences. We started out with a tent and had lots of fun. Then my mum and dad bought a motorhome. I loved it. It was a far cry from our tent and I could see how much more convenient holidays could be.

"We quickly saw a vehicle we liked and went for it... And we haven't looked back. We have more freedom than we did with a tent, and our inflatable awning means we have just as much space - and it's a lot simpler to set up camp.

"Our first trip in our camper was to West Wittering Beach in Sussex. It was beautiful. We enjoyed glorious views of Chichester Harbour and the South Downs, and parking was easy because of the acres of grass near the beach. We even had a picnic in the campervan.

"Our first real holiday was to the Ardèche in the South of France. This involved a lot of driving, but even that was fun because we made the travelling part of the adventure. We spent five days travelling down - stopping at places that took our fancy. The kids loved it and it was so easy compared to the tent. Instead, we just parked up and when it was time to leave the next day we were ready in minutes, not hours.

"One of our best experiences was a campsite in the Cévennes mountains. We swam in the river every day and watched the beavers in the evening. We parked next to the river, and all this was just outside the campervan door! You can imagine my kids' reactions - it's something we'll never forget. We went gold panning and were lucky enough to find some. That was exciting - the look on their faces was brilliant.

"We've got packing the van off to a fine art now. Surprisingly, the most useful thing is our levellers. With these, it's easy to turn a wonky pitch into somewhere perfect to spend the night. It's impossible to sleep on a steep slope.

"We've also learnt to put a full kettle on the hob before we go to bed. In France, a van came round with fresh croissants on the first day our holiday, but we had to put the bed away to reach the kettle - so no breakfast in bed for us! Needless to say we didn't make the same mistake again.

"We all love owning a campervan; we've had brilliant times as a family and it feels good to know that I've invested in my children's memories."

Kieron's family enjoy making memories in their camper

Chapter 12

Canine capers

The secrets of dog-friendly campervan adventures

If you're a dog owner, holidays can be tricky. Few hotels and bed and breakfast places welcome dogs in their rooms, which can mean putting your 'best friend' in kennels while you're away.

If you have a campervan you can take your dog with you. This is easy if you're travelling in the UK and if you get a pet passport, you can take your pet dog or cat abroad (see *www.gov.uk/take-pet-abroad*).

You know your dog's temperament and whether they need to be harnessed or put in a container for travel. You certainly don't want them to go running off each time you stop for a break.

Cathie keeps things simple with her Collie Cross. She says:

"She's quite calm now she's older and she just sleeps in her bed in the centre of the campervan, behind the cab seats. Sometimes I sleep in the inflatable drive-away awning with her, in the summer. I can't let her sleep out there on her own. I can put the awning up on my own.

The interior of my CamperCar is mostly grey, with Noma Rustic wood-effect flooring that doesn't seem to show the sand or the mud too much."

Other people ask us to customise their campervans to make travelling with pets safe and easy, and many campsites offer dog walking routes and even dog showers, making you feel welcome when you arrive at your destination.

Here are some top tips for travelling and camping in style with your pet.

Sufficient space for your dog?

You have a few options. Many campervan owners put their dogs in a cage or a crate during the drive, while others opt for a dog seat belt. Some dogs will happily sit in their bed in the back. It really depends on your animal and the space you have available.

If your pet travels in a cage or crate, then you'll want to secure it inside your van. Take it with you when choosing your campervan, to gauge the size of vehicle you need.

Remember, it's not just how much space the crate takes up, it's also how you plan to use your vehicle. Will your dog also sleep in the crate? If so, you'll want to design your campervan so the crate isn't in the way during the daytime. We've found that incorporating the crate into the back of the vehicle works best in rear kitchen models.

When it comes to securing your crate, it's possible to install special rings in the floor of your vehicle, so you can strap it down for travel. That way you won't need to worry about your dog's safety when you're on the road.

Interior design

Many off-the-peg vehicles have light coloured interiors. This is a challenge if you have a dog, as every speck of dirt will show up and the upholstery can be harder to keep looking clean. With a customised interior you can choose the colour of your soft furnishings. It's worth considering a light charcoal, or even something darker, that won't show the paw prints too much.

Choose wipe-clean vinyl flooring, instead of carpet. If your dog moults easily, a hard floor is easier to keep free of dog hairs.

Tips for travelling with dogs

If your dog is happy travelling in a car, he'll be comfortable in the campervan. He may even prefer the camper as it will feel more spacious. In fact, don't be surprised if your dog ends up loving the campervan as much as you do - after all, this is a great opportunity for them to spend more time with their favourite person, getting more walks and extra petting. You'll tend to be more relaxed on holiday, so your dog will feel more relaxed too.

When you head off on an adventure, we suggest planning in some stops to give your dog a chance to stretch its legs. This is so easy in your campervan. Once you've found a scenic spot, simply pull over and brew yourself a cuppa at the same time. Bliss.

Some dog owners like to acclimatise their dog to the campervan before heading out on a longer trip. This will help you figure out what your pet needs to feel most

We built custom dog cages to keep Penny's Westies safe on the road in her VW Caledonia

comfortable. So maybe you could head to the beach and reward your dog with a long walk.

Don't forget the dog owner's travel essentials:

- Travel water bowl and a food bowl - make sure water is available at all times (this is easy in a campervan because you have water on tap)
- Their usual food and treats
- A plastic mat to go under the bowls

- Dog brush
- Dog poo bags
- Collapsing silicone bucket for paw washing
- Old towels to dry your dog (microfibre ones dry quickly)
- Shampoo for washing a muddy dog
- Dog toys
- Disinfectant spray

Another tip: try training your dog to only use the side habitation doors. You could even block access to the front cab. That way, if you open the cab or the rear door, they won't automatically see it as an invitation to leave the vehicle.

Stress-free camping

If you've chosen a campsite that welcomes dogs (most do), you may find dog-friendly facilities, like a dog walking area.

When you arrive, it's worth checking for any restrictions. Do you need to keep your dog on the lead? Other rules

Ben the Mastiff approved of his owner's campervan

are common sense, such as cleaning up any dog mess. Regardless, your dog will love being with you and discovering the new smells of a new place.

When it comes to sleeping, each dog owner will simply find their own way. It's worth bringing the cushion, toy or blanket that your dog sleeps with at home. They'll feel reassured and comforted by its familiarity. Your dog could sleep in its travel cage or in the awning. Alternatively, some owners like to have a special cubby hole created under the bed for their pet's bed.

To get the best night sleep, we find that it helps to get into a routine. Our dog, Angus, gets a good walk and a pee before he goes to bed. Then we wash and dry his feet to keep the campervan cleaner. After that, he'll happily drift off.

During the day

Have you noticed that dogs seem to have their own alarm clock that tells them when they should be been fed or walked? We try to keep Angus' routine as close to what he experiences at home. This helps him to feel more relaxed and settled.

Barney jumped straight in and got comfy when his owners collected their Manhattan MPV campervan

- We take our dog out for their walk at the same time as at home.

- We feed our dog at the same time as normal.

Barking can be a problem. Angus is a West Highland Terrier and tends to bark and patrol his zone. There are ways to prevent this on a campsite, so we don't annoy our fellow campers. We use windbreaks to create a zone for our dog that's exclusively ours.

Pebbles likes sitting on a non-slip mat for travel

We take Angus for a walk all around the campsite on arrival. He can have a nosy peek at everyone else and get familiar with his new surroundings.

Assuming it's nice and cool and the roof is up, your dog may be happy to sit in the campervan, but it's likely he'll prefer to be outside.

If that's the case, we can only suggest that you get yourself set up so your dog can't wander off. Not all campers like dogs.

Angus is a wanderer. He loves to join in the fun and play with our children, barking excitedly. We tether him to a corkscrew peg using his lead, giving him some freedom but not letting him run off.

Tips for dog owners

- Create a run for your dog using windbreaks. Our kids love to get Angus to run up and down, while cheering him on, and we like to sit watching them, while enjoying a cuppa

- Keep a selection of your dog's favourite toys permanently in the campervan. That way you always have something to occupy your pet, without having to remember to pack them

- Try playing tennis on a string - it's our dog's favourite game. This game folds up small for storage in the camper.

What to do with a muddy dog

Angus has a passion for water, so if he sees a nice lake or pond then in he goes. As a result, his white fur turns various shades of grey and brown.

We always choose a hardstanding pitch, if there's one available. Grass pitches get wet underfoot, which can make your dog extra muddy.

If your dog tends to get muddy, consider taking a separate water bottle with a shower attached in the back your vehicle. A plant spray will do. Use this to rinse mud and grime off your dog's fur. Finish off with a vigorous towel rub and everyone will be happy.

As a bonus, you can clean off your wellies with the dog shower, as well.

A dog anchor keeps Barney from wandering too far

'Heelwork to music' is the proper name for Penny's hobby, and she's discovered that life is sweeter on the road with her two Westies, now she has her VW Caledonia

"I used to go to weekend 'Heelwork to music' obedience training events with my dogs Harry and Jasper, in a little VW Caddy van. It was not relaxing setting up camp and packing it all away Dog events involve long days waiting around, taking part and competing, and we all ended up tired. I looked at big tents, but then I fell in love with campervans.

"I bought the VW Caledonia from Sussex Campervans, customised with built-in dog crates, in March 2017, and it's made the events far more comfortable. The dogs relax far more than they used to - as soon as they're inside, they just go to sleep.

I've taken them all around Britain: Scotland, Yorkshire, the Midlands, Blackpool, Kent and Sussex. Next year I'm going to Gloucester and Wales."

Penny packs less these days, "Having a campervan makes preparing for a trip easier; lots of items live in the camper all the time. The week before a trip, I might pack the clothes into the cupboard one night, and other things another night. Then I just call into Marks and Spencer on the way, and get ingredients for that day's meals. I have decided to remove my dried food from the campervan, because I'm just not using it. I'm seldom somewhere completely remote. There is one food that doesn't travel well, but I have the solution: my bananas now travel in the sink."

What are Penny's top tips for people new to touring with dogs? She says, "The pop-top in the campervan is really handy, because I can store things out of reach of the dogs. I keep a small collapsible waste bin up there, and empty it frequently. The dogs mostly eat dried dog food, measured out into portions for each dog before we go. I put them into plastic bags sealed with clips.

"Jasper, who is three, is the escape artist, but Harry, 13, is calmer. I have Cornish mesh windbreaks, so the dogs can see through it. Jasper can wriggle under the awning skirt, so I have bought low border fencing for gardens, to stop him from escaping.

"The dogs took to the camper immediately. Jasper can jump in, while Harry uses my £20 collapsible step to get in. It has a mesh top, so water drains through, yet it's sturdy enough for my 83-year-old mother to use. To get the dogs into their crates for safer travelling, I do encourage them with food treats. They now jump in the van and then wait for the treats before they'll go to bed in the crates. I always have plenty of treats for them. Dogs are like children, they're fine if you keep to a regular rhythm. Once we're parked up, they sleep on the bed with me.

"I always keep a dark coloured blanket on the end of the bed. After a muddy walk, if the dogs jump on the bed it

Jasper and Harry can watch through the netting

Penny has a custom pop-top cover for extra insulation at winter dog shows - even when it was -2°c outside, the camper stayed cosy

won't ruin your bedding. I also bought rubber-backed washable mats to absorb wet paw prints near the side door of the camper. Then I made a fly screen for the side door, hanging it on the awning bracket. I made it by adding Velcro and hem weights to three panels of cheap black netting screens that I bought from Lidl. It came with magnets in the centre and sides, so it 'sticks' to the van. It cost me about £10."

When she's not off to dog obedience weekends, Penny uses her campervan to visit her sister and her children, camping on the drive. She says, "My mother has a bad back, so when we go out in the camper she can stretch out properly for a nap, while I walk the dogs.

"I even use the campervan for holidays. I got together with a group of friends last year and we went up to Harrogate. It was nice to relax."

Chapter 13

Maintenance made simple

Here are some easy ways to look after your campervan

Campervans are robust, but you do need to take care of them. If you're new to camping, there may be equipment that's unfamiliar to you. Do you know how to change a gas bottle in a standard campervan? How do you know it's safe? How do you keep your campervan clean? Read on for our top tips.

Safe travelling

Your campervan is first and foremost a motor vehicle and it's up to you to make sure it's safe to drive. Here's a simple pre-trip campervan checklist:

- Check the oil, water and fluids in your campervan and top up where necessary
- Check the condition of your tyres and ensure they're inflated to the correct pressure
- Check the spare wheel is inflated and is legal
- Take the key to the locking wheel nuts, just in case.
- Check wiper blades

- Ensure the leisure battery is charged at least a day before the trip
- Turn off the gas by turning the valve on the top. If you have an LPG tank mounted under the campervan for your heating and hob, you may be able to switch the gas off simply by using the control panel
- Turn the water pump off
- Put the table up, and place the bed in the seat position
- Close the lids on the sink and hob unit
- If you have a pop-up roof, pull it down and secure it with the clips or straps provided, and check all round the outside
- If you were hooked up to the mains, remove the cable, coil it up and place it in the camper.

Daniel took this VW Caledonia to Brighton in February - campervans really can be used all year round

Maintenance equipment list

With luck, you won't have to do anything on the road. But just in case, we take these items.

- An old towel to lie on
- Basic tools such as screwdrivers and spanners
- A wooden mallet for a windbreak or awning pegs
- A torch
- Duct tape (ideal for makeshift repairs
- Superglue
- Disposable gloves
- A few spare fuses, just in case

Powering your living space

Most campervans use both gas and electricity. They provide both standard household sockets and USB/12V sockets. This means you can still use many of your favourite appliances and gadgets on holiday. So, how are these sockets powered?

- Your vehicle and leisure batteries
- Mains hook-up

The main difference is that your 240V standard plug sockets will only work when hooked up to the mains, unless you have the latest inverter tech.

Two batteries

Your campervan may have two batteries, which require no maintenance.

- The car battery, which starts your vehicle and powers the headlamps, cab lights, and radio.
- The leisure battery, which powers the 12V and USB sockets, the LED lighting, the fridge-freezer and the water pump.

The fridge-freezer generally runs on 12 Volts, so it will work whether you're on an electrical hook-up or not. The battery will keep it going for a while without being charged.

12 Volt sockets are surprisingly useful. Camping and motoring accessory shops sell low-powered 12 Volt appliances like travel kettles, coolboxes, slow cookers, electric griddles, toasters, electric hobs, heaters, fans, hair straighteners and hairdryers.

Both batteries should automatically charge when the vehicle is driven or when you plug the campervan into the mains. In addition, you can charge your leisure battery at home by plugging it into a 240V socket using a special adapter cable.

Electric hook-up

Most campsites provide a mains electricity hook-up post for each of the hardstanding pitches, so that you can use your orange hook-up cable to connect your campervan to the mains electricity supply.

Once hooked up, you can use the 240V sockets to run normal household appliances like a microwave or slow cooker, phone charger, hairdryer or laptop.

The mains supply will also power everything else in your vehicle and give your leisure battery a rest while it is being recharged.

Here's how to connect your hook-up cable. Pull it out and identify each end. One is open-ended and one has a cap. Push the pins of the open end into the electric hook-up socket.

Campsite electrics make it possible to use normal appliances

The capped end plugs into the campervan's electric hook-up 'plug socket', usually on the off-side of the vehicle. Open the hatch, line up the pins and holes and push the cable plug into the socket.

When you drive off, remember to unhook and coil up the cable and store it in your van.

Gas

Gas runs the hob burners and operates any gas heating. We use our gas bottle to operate a gas BBQ, too. In most campervans you'll need a gas bottle, connected and turned on.

How to fit and operate your gas bottle - no tools required!

1. Inside the gas cupboard you'll see a strap and the 'pigtail' connector.

2. Place the bottle inside the cupboard, making sure you have access to the two black straps.

3. Align the connector with the socket in the top of the bottle and turn the pigtail end to connect them. It's

Time to swap an empty gas bottle for a full one

a left-hand thread, so turn anti-clockwise. Use a spanner and leak detector fluid.

If you have any issues installing the bottle, consult the gas supplier.

4. Once the gas bottle is connected, tighten the black securing straps.

5. If the gas cupboard won't close, twist the gas bottle until the pipe is inside neatly and check it's not trapped.

6. Remember to turn off the regulator on top of the gas bottle when you're driving. This is even more important when you go on a ferry or to France through EuroTunnel.

It's critical your gas is safely installed and meets all the relevant gas regulations. The gas cupboard should be sealed to the inside of the van and vented outside, which means that in the event of a leak, there's no danger to you from the fumes.

When you're out and about, a common question is "how much gas is left?" After all, you don't want to be cut off halfway through cooking your evening's feast! There are gauges you can buy - but we've not found them to be too reliable. We rely on the 'swish test'. Give the bottle a shake. If it has a bit of 'swish' you'll have another night left - at least. No swish or movement, then your bottle is empty.

New LPG tanks and solar systems are in…

A few of the latest campervans, such as those at Sussex Campervans, now have LPG tanks mounted under the body of the van, powering the heating and hob. These are better than the traditional gas bottles, because they are mounted outside the vehicle and controlled from inside the vehicle, using a simple control panel.

You can turn the LPG off for travel with a press of the button, and turn it on again when you're parked up, just as easily. On the control panel there's also a gauge to tell you when you need to top the LPG tank up (LPG is sold at many motorway and A-road petrol stations). These LPG tanks are a good size, so they'll keep you going for longer than Camping Gaz, and there's a simple external filler cap with adjacent barbecue point. You'll never have to disconnect them to fill them up with gas. And you don't need to wait until the tank is empty - you can top it up at any time, without loss.

Solar panels are also available as an option, and these do a surprising amount to keep your leisure battery charged up, even in the winter.

How to use your gas hob
Campervan hobs tend to come with two gas rings and an igniter.

To light a ring, start the flow of gas by turning the knob and push the ignition button. Hold the gas knob in for a few seconds until the flame is steady. Then control the size of the flame by twisting the knob. Simple.

Onboard heating
Run off your gas bottle or LPG tank, an on-board heater helps keep your camper toasty warm when you're pitched up on those cold winter nights. Most of them are 'blown air' heaters, mounted under the vehicle, under a seat or within the furniture, blowing air into the campervan, through a vent at low level.

Water
You can have running water in most campervans, thanks to an onboard water container, the sink and taps, and your water pump.

You'll need to drop your submersible water pump into the water container once you've filled it up, as this is the gadget that delivers water to your tap. It requires electricity, but you can leave the pump on all the time. That's because the pump will only use power when the tap is open.

When you empty the sink, the wastewater will drain to an outlet, usually on the offside. Put a bowl or bucket under the outlet if you're on a campsite, then dispose of it responsibly. Campsites have a waste disposal area for 'grey' water.

Your onboard toilet
When you're away, you need to look after your cassette toilet in much the same way as your toilet at home. Empty it when full and keep it clean using some bathroom spray.

After your holiday, empty out all the chemicals and flush them down your toilet at home. If you have a septic tank, use eco-friendly toilet chemicals or empty the loo at the campsite before you leave.

The portable loo has a rubber seal. If you use a little silicone spray on the seal, it will help it close properly for years to come.

Winter checklist

When the winter descends, you may find your camper sits a little longer on your driveway. Here's how we winterise our camper.

Water

- Switch off the water pump and pull the pump and pipes out of the water tank. Allow them to hang loose in the cupboard.

Drain the water out of your camper if the weather gets icy

- Empty the water container, leave it to drain for a while, then place back in the cupboard without the seal or the lid on.
- Switch the pump off at the power control panel and open the tap in the sink to prevent water getting into the pipes.

Not only does this help prevent any frost damage, but it allows the pipes and water container to air out, reducing the risk of mould or stale water in your containers.

Fridge

- Turn off the fridge.
- If your fridge has an aerator, use this to stop the fridge door closing entirely. Alternatively just leave the fridge door open.

This allows air to get in and helps prevent mildew or nasty smells.

Gas

- Switch off gas on the bottle.
- Or, switch off the gas on the control panel (if you have an LPG tank mounted beneath the vehicle).

Show it some love

Pop the top occasionally, open the vents, and air out your van. Why not have a cup of tea in it?

Turn the engine on now and again and let it run for 20 minutes. Even better, drive it to see a friend, go out for lunch, or visit a park.

Regular maintenance

As your campervan is a motor vehicle, normal requirements for servicing and maintenance apply.

Three years after its first registration, every vehicle in the UK will be MOT tested annually, and this will show up any points needing attention. In addition, to keep your vehicle running smoothly and keep your warranty valid, you should get the vehicle serviced in line with the manufacturer's required service intervals. This will involve changing the oil, air filter, cabin filter, and other parts.

Unlike a car, your campervan is also required to have an annual habitation check, to maintain the van converter's warranty. Most importantly, the converter will check that the gas supply and electricity remain safe. in addition, the check will review the water system and look out for signs of damp. Many other items will also be checked, and it's always best if any problems are identified early, to prevent any further damage.

Your campervan is your home from home, so it pays to keep the fixtures and fittings clean and free from dust and dirt and lubricate any hinges. We use a light spray of furniture polish on internal surfaces and upholstery cleaner for any trimming and upholstery. We clean it on a dry day and air it out afterwards.

Hinges and moving parts should be kept clean and lubricated. We use oil or WD40 to do this.

With the hinges of your pop-top roof or the base of your cab swivel seat, simply give them a quick squirt of silicone spray occasionally.

If curtain rails become sticky in time and don't slide open and shut so easily, lubricate the runners with silicone spray and they feel like new.

Once the maintenance is done, you deserve a holiday - Bill & Elsa enjoy heading to France

Chapter 14

Choosing the right campervan for you

A modern van conversion gives you a nimble family car, a mobile café and a home on wheels

Unlike larger coachbuilt motorhomes, van conversions are easier to drive and have better fuel economy. This makes them ideal for people who want to use them as their only vehicle, as well a for day trips, weekends, and holidays.

Once you've decided to embrace the campervan lifestyle, how do you choose the right campervan for you? It's a big investment, so you want to find a vehicle that works for all your needs.

Campervan versus RV or coachbuilt motorhome

It's true, you would have more space if you bought an American RV or a coachbuilt motorhome. In our experience, these chunkier models feel as though you're driving a 'block of flats on wheels' - they end up on the drive for most of the year.

The footprint of a modern campervan is similar in size to a large car, which means they are easy to drive and park. So, you're far more likely to 'just go' - especially given the fuel economy of modern vehicles.

There are a few factory-built campervans on the market, such as the Volkswagen California, but there are far more van conversions.

A conversion is a commercial 'panel van' vehicle, which has been 'converted' into a camper by adding a sleeping, cooking and living space in the back. Built by expert campervan converters or campervan builders, this type of leisure vehicle offers good fuel economy, as well as being easy to maintain and repair. Unlike caravans and coachbuilt motorhomes, damp is rarely an issue, because the vehicle has a metal body.

The key benefit of a van conversion over a factory-built model is the flexibility you have over the interior. Some specialist van converters will allow you to adapt their interior to suit your needs. This kind of bespoke interior means fewer compromises - so you'll love and use your campervan even more.

New or old?

Once you've decided to invest in a van conversion, you have two choices:

1. Ask your converter to buy a brand new vehicle to convert for you

Choose your preferred layout and the rest will follow

2. Ask your converter to buy a used vehicle to convert. We call this 'brand new secondhand'.

A 'brand new secondhand' conversion is a new interior fitted into a quality used panel van, bought from a reliable source. The interior includes windows, insulation, trimming, plumbing, electrics, gas installation, appliances, sockets, lighting, beds, upholstery, cupboards, a table and an elevating pop-top roof. They have a feel of a new vehicle, but cost less.

The birth of a campervan

From start to finish, it takes a few weeks to convert a vehicle into a campervan. Here's a quick overview of the transformation process.

- Source the perfect vehicle for the client, get it valeted and serviced on arrival
- Design the interior layout to meet the client's needs, based on the current range
- Choose from an array of upholstery fabrics and furniture woods to create an attractive interior
- Cut the fabric to pattern

- CNC cut the furniture panels accurately to size
- Prepare the vehicle and fit the pop-top roof and windows
- Install gas and electrics
- Install insulation. We trim every surface with carpet for extra warmth and to ensure no unsightly metal is visible
- Seal the windows to make the vehicle air and wind tight and we usually add privacy glass
- Lay hard-wearing vinyl on the floor
- Assemble the furniture, including seats/beds, storage space, and the table
- Wire in the fridge and install the hob, sink and heater
- Make the pop-up roof tent (in a dark colour to blackout)
- Fit blackout curtains
- Test the vehicle robustly

A VW is the classic choice for a campervan

- Give the new owners a thorough handover
- Now, let the fun begin!

What vehicle should you choose?

Arguably, the base vehicle is the most important choice of all. So which van should you pick?

Buy the best base vehicle you can afford. A high quality new or nearly new vehicle is likely to be more reliable and last longer than something cheap. While the conversion process will make the interior look brand new, you don't want to waste money on a vehicle that doesn't perform.

We've been converting and testing vans since 2010, and we've found the following vehicles are about the best when it comes to combining space, with reliability, and manoeuvrability. Any of the following would make a brilliant campervan.

Volkswagen Transporter

Since the birth of the iconic VW splitscreen bus or 'splitty', a Volkswagen remains one of the most popular choices for a campervan conversion. To many people the VW is the iconic camper, right down to the chrome VW badge on the front. Volkswagen even builds its own factory conversion - the VW California.

The modern VW Transporter T6 van converts into a fine campervan. Available in two lengths, it's an excellent base vehicle and the common rail diesel engine makes for a superb crisp 'Germanic' drive.

Renault Trafic or the Nissan NV300

These vans are closely related, and also convert into superb campervans. You can choose a pop-top elevating roof campervan or a high-top version.

The low engine noise and smooth suspension makes this trio of vehicles supremely comfortable to drive.

The vans were created as a joint venture between GM, Renault and Nissan. Current models feature the latest 'Bi-Turbo' diesel technology, a Renault-engineered 2.0-litre Diesel engine, with a six-speed manual gearbox.

Like the VW T6, there are two versions. The short-wheelbase option is roughly the same size externally as the VW T6 at 'waist' level, but has more vertical sides. This increases the internal volume without requiring a

These vehicles have won awards and are easy to drive

bigger footprint. The long-wheelbase (LWB) version offers a little more length to the accommodation inside.

Compact campervans

If you're only sleeping one or two people in your van, you can afford to go even smaller with your vehicle. Until recently, the Citroën C15 or Citroën Berlingo with a Romahome-type conversion, or Bambi-type conversion on the Suzuki Carry microvan was a popular choice.

I was driving down the M1 when I spotted a nimble looking van on the other carriageway that made me turn my head. It looked just like a Volkswagen van that had shrunk in the wash! I did some research and discovered that it was a Nissan NV200. The vehicle isn't based on a car - like most smaller vans. Instead, it has been specially designed. My instinct told me this vehicle would make a perfect campervan, and so I bought one to experiment with.

The Nissan NV200 CamperCar is deceptively roomy and easy to drive. It looks like a campervan which has been expertly 'shrunk' down to a more convenient size. It's only slightly bigger than a small car, which makes

ur CamperCar is based on the reliable Nissan NV200

parking a doddle. And unbelievably it still holds up to four people. As a result, it can be used as a car as well as a campervan. And with the 1.5DCi engine you get incredible fuel economy.

We've converted the Nissan NV200 with our own custom-designed elevating roof, to make a small pop-top campervan - our CamperCar. It's astonishing just how practical this small vehicle can be.

What to fit in your interior

Once you've chosen your base vehicle, the next step is to plan the all-important interior.

While the campervanning lifestyle is all about freedom, adventure, and the open road, it's also about individuality. And that's the real joy of a custom-built conversion.

After all, a family will have different needs to a couple. Similarly, a surfer will have different space requirements to an elderly couple who want room to relax.

With a custom conversion, you could order:

- Beds for up to five people

- A rear kitchen layout for extra privacy
- Extra shelves in the cupboards
- A toilet cubicle
- Extra sockets for convenience
- Your choice of fabric trimmings for the seats and beds
- Your choice of a wide selection of furniture colours for the perfect finish.

A good campervan conversion maintains a balance between functionality and comfort. So, you must ensure the seats not only ensure safe travel, but allow you to travel long distances without aches and pains. Equally, they will become a bed at the end of a busy day.

As well as comfort at night, there's the layout itself - you don't want to feel cramped.

This is where interior design plays a key role. To maximise the available space, we put lots of storage in our campers, as well as the beds, table, seats, sink, cupboards, portable loo, etc. With clever design you'll enjoy a generous living area.

Safety and comfort

As you'll be sleeping and cooking in your campervan as well as driving, you'll want the reassurance that your conversion is safe.

Converting vehicles is a specialist job - and there are essential safety requirements, too.

- Mains electrical work should comply with BS 7671: 17th Edition Wiring Regulations
- Gas installations should comply with BS EN 1949
- 12V electrics should comply with BS EN 1648
- Habitation specification to BS EN 1646

It sounds as if there's a lot to consider, but when you choose the right campervan converter you'll find that they make the process straightforward and fun.

Therapist Sue has owned her Bamboo Green Paradise Twin for less than a year, yet she and her husband Rick have already explored large parts of Europe in it

Sue says, "We picked the campervan up and went off for three weeks to France, Switzerland, Italy, Spain and back home through France. It was a very good trip and we stayed in an olive grove and visited a nice old hotel made from former stables at San Guiliano, near Pisa in Italy. Then, later in the year we went to Dorset for a break as well.

"We were originally tent campers but we wanted more comfort. We leave our dog Ted with friends and spend summers visiting our son in Canada. So we promised Ted, who is a Bedlington terrier, that the deal is that we would take him away in the campervan whenever we were not in Canada.

"I work as a therapist, so I can restructure my life so that I can get more holidays than most people. We travel with friends and they sleep in little tents, with our awning as the social hub. Soon, we're going to Spain and meeting a friend who lives out there."

Parking considerations can determine the type of campervan that you buy, says Sue. "We live on busy Lewes High Street, in Sussex, where there's hardly any residents' parking space. Thankfully, our daughter has a flat with underground parking, and our campervan just fits in.

"I love the smell of our campervan, it's so evocative of holidays. The bed is just wonderful. We are both big and tall people so our bed in the Paradise Twin campervan is heaven and it fits us and Ted as well. He has an excuse to sleep with us when we're away. The blackout curtains are excellent - I sleep so well in this campervan."

It's sunny all year round in Sue & Rick's colourful camper

Jim and Joy use their Manhattan MPV to explore the UK, towing their beloved 45-year-old MG Midget behind

Now retired, Jim and Joy have the freedom to head off on adventures whenever they choose. They had always enjoyed the outdoors when they were younger. Since they bought their Panorama Blue Manhattan MPV campervan in 2015, they have travelled extensively in the UK and met up with friends all over Europe.

Jim says, "We have a lot of friends who enjoy camping - some of whom we've known since our tenting days in the 1970s. Once a year we meet up with a with a group of former colleagues, and we're always heading off to visit friends.

"The campervan makes this so easy. It's a joy to drive, so journeys are always fun – better than in our car. And if friends don't have a spare room, we can sleep in our vehicle. We love having the independence and freedom to do what we like."

Jim also owns a beautifully restored 45-year-old MG Midget, which he loves to drive and takes to rallies. The camper's economy is fabulous for towing and provides flexibility when they are away.

The Manhattan can tow the Midget on a trailer, which means Jim and Joy can leave the campervan parked up and explore the local area in the Midget. The car becomes a real asset when they are staying in one place for an extended period of time.

Jim & Joy sent us this photo from the Pyrenees

Jim's beloved MG Midget goes on holiday with them, too

On MG race days, Jim arrives early and spends the night in his campervan, so he's properly refreshed before hitting the tracks.

Jim and Joy say that their campervan is helping them make the most of their retirement. "It's so carefree, with a campervan. Sometimes we'll book some campsites ahead. For example, when we went to the Outer Hebrides we booked the first two nights, because we weren't sure what was available. Then we just went where our noses took us.

"It's fantastic being able to toss a coin at the end of the driveway and use that to decide if we'll turn left or right. We've already planned our next adventure and we are simply loving it."

171

Chapter 15

Travellers' tales: stories from the open road

How do you use your campervan? We asked our friends - and the answers were as varied as the individuals themselves. Sit back, relax and enjoy a few road trips with campervan owners

Investing Alan's redundancy money in a campervan has allowed them to spend more time visiting friends

Alan and Sue use their campervan for an active retirement with their beautiful Labradoodle, Barney

Alan says "I thought about owning a campervan for years before I actually took the plunge. My friend had bought one, and I had decided that I wanted to buy a camper when I retired.

"I ended up taking early redundancy and realised I had enough cash to buy a campervan. I did think about buying a Porsche instead for a while, but I settled on the campervan and it's been the best thing I've ever bought. I love driving it - even if I'm stuck in traffic. The campervan is comfortable and I like being able to see above the cars.

"Sue loves it too. We had a trailer tent when the kids were growing up, so we were no strangers to camping. Sue and I have been on lots of package holidays over the years, so we were ready to do something different in our retirement. We decided to explore more of the UK.

"Our gorgeous Labradoodle, Barney loves to come with us too. He's a great traveller and happily sits in his cage while we are travelling along. He used to sleep under the bed, but he now joins us. Yes, a campervan bed is big enough for two adults and a very big fluffy dog.

"The campervan is brilliant for Barney and he just adds to the adventure for us. He loves running up and down the beaches, and because he is such a lovely looking dog, he attracts lots of attention.

"Our campervan has shaped our lifestyle and encouraged us to get in touch with old friends. We went up to Scotland to see one of my wife's friends who she's not seen for 50 years. It was brilliant seeing them together. Time evaporated, and they are now really good friends again. We would never have done this without the campervan.

"We've had lots of great adventures. While we were in Scotland we drove the North Coast 500. It's an amazing road that winds up through the mountains. The scenery was absolutely stunning. If we saw somewhere

With all they need on board, they can go anywhere

points in Britain, it's only right that I should finish off the compass now.

"Our campervan also allows me to spend lovely times with Sue. We always have a good time; it's just so easy. We simply pull up at a site, pop up the awning and we're on holiday. And, because we try to stay within walking distance of a pub or a restaurant, we get to enjoy lots of nice meals together too. Our campervan is the best thing I ever bought."

Three years later...

Alan and Sue are still having a great time in their campervan. Alan gave us an update:

"I like to walk along the coast on a cold winter's day, then get back into the van, have a hot cup of tea with fish and chips and watch the waves breaking out at sea, while we are warm and cosy inside. Whether it's just a day out or a longer trip away it's always fun in the van.

"Our next planned adventure is to the Peak District, but I'm sure we'll be away somewhere before then. Being retired makes life easier and simpler; enjoy it while you can - I know we do."

particularly beautiful, we could pull over and have a cup of tea or coffee.

"We have lots planned for future trips. I want to go to Lowestoft as it's the most easterly point in the UK. After visiting the most northerly, southerly, and westerly

Alex & Sue found this campsite in Inverness - what a spectacular location!

Shrimp the whippet sits happily between Geoff and Jane in the cab of their campervan for their adventures

"Jane takes the car and I use the camper to get to work. I do property inspections. My patch is quite large, from Dover in Kent to Brize Norton in West Oxfordshire, so I'm glad the campervan is so easy to drive and park. I'm retiring soon, so I'm looking forward to using it even more this year."

Shrimp the navigator

Did they have any difficulty getting their dog used to the campervan? Geoff laughs, "No, Shrimp jumped straight into the middle of the front seat, before we had time to decide where she should go. We clip her harness to the middle seat belt and she checks that we're following the satnav correctly.

"At night she sleeps on the front cab seat, but sometimes sneaks onto our Rock 'n' Roll bed. She's so good at hiding - if we leave the bed down, she burrows under the bedding, so we can't see her."

Dog walking and day trips

Does the campervan have any other uses? "Yes, dog walks" says Geoff.

"We are National Trust members, and we take the campervan so we can make a hot drink in the car park. It's a lot more comfy than sitting in a car if the weather is bad. It's also very sociable when you're in a campervan. People come up to talk to us and ask if they can have a look inside. They're always amazed to discover that it's possible to choose the upholstery and furniture inside."

Planning a 'Grand Tour'

"I'm looking forward to retirement, and friends have bought a place in Puglia, Southern Italy, so we're going away for four or five weeks. I think we'll head for Annecy and go through the Mont Blanc Tunnel. My grandfather is from Italy so we might visit his village in search of my family history. He came to live in London in his 20s, and

Shrimp has her favourite seat in the campervan

married my grandmother, who was also Italian. I wish I'd asked more about where he grew up."

No stress

Geoff and Jane have had a busy first year, and they know everything gets easier with practice. Geoff says, "At one French campsite a Dutch family were towing a caravan with their campervan. Two slept in the caravan, and two in the camper. I couldn't believe how quickly they packed up and drove off in the morning; they're obviously very experienced."

Most rookie errors turn out fine. Geoff says,"We drive for up to four hours a day, but I forgot the hour's time difference last time. We left the UK at midday and the Tunnel takes less than an hour, but we arrived in France at 2pm. We had planned a night in the Loire, but as it was late I just asked Jane to look on her phone for the nearest campsite. There was no stress involved."

Accessories keep multiplying...

Geoff says "You do have to be careful not to buy too many gadgets, or you will clutter the campervan. We bought a Cadac barbecue - they're good. We went to the NEC show and bought a TV. You can record the TV at home, then take it with you to watch them abroad.

However prudent Jane and Geoff's purchases might be, friends and family members can't resist joining in with the fun. Geoff says, "Christmas presents have become easy for our family now - they all revolve around the campervan.

"My daughter had a washable doormat printed for us, with the words: 'All welcome as long as you have a bottle of Prosecco and a treat for Shrimp'. We've also received campsite guide books and The Camper's Wine Trail book from friends and family - which will actually be very useful."

Geoff and Jane enjoy the freedom of campervan life

Melanie has a Manhattan SWB campervan called Buttercup. She's currently 'living the dream' in France

Mel's camper has the classic side-kitchen layout.

"We've had our campervan since July 2015 and we also rent a cottage in the South of France to use as our base. We spend a lot of time in France - it was all part of our dream, along with getting a camper.

"Buttercup the campervan is the perfect everyday vehicle, as well as our ticket to explore more of this beautiful country. We go out all the time in the Manhattan, from a few days of wild camping to weeks of exploring during the summer in France and around Europe.

"We're both very active and love having the camper because it gives us so much freedom. We prefer to just have the top up so we can stand up and cook on the stove. Then the seats fold down to a large double bed - it's very cosy, especially after years of going camping in a tent in Wales."

For Melanie, owning a campervan means freedom

Ever since she bought her Nissan CamperCar as her only vehicle, Ruth has found that it improves life in many ways

She says, "My campervan is my only vehicle, and it saves me lots of money at motorway service stations - I just park up and make a drink, without paying through the nose for a tea or a coffee, or I can choose a lay-by with a stunning view.

"One major thing - there are a lot of journeys that I used to do in one day but now I'm 64 I get so tired. These days I break the journey with a night stop and have two pleasant days instead of one stressed one and one shattered one.

"I've worked out where the good stopping places are on the journeys I do frequently; designated picnic areas are good, as are Forestry Commision car parks. On the second day, I can stop and explore interesting towns if I want to.

"I haven't got a garden, because I live in a flat in Brighton, so I use my campervan for mini-outings.

Where someone else might use their garden on a fine day, I will often go out - there are a few pleasant places near Brighton where you can park conveniently. I can get in the back of the camper, open the side door and sit reading and having a cup of tea with a sea view."

Holidays off-grid

Ruth likes to get away from it all, she says, "I use the camper to go to a women's co-operative in Wales. I love going there, but things are pretty low-tech and I have nicknamed the visitors' cottage 'ice-cube cottage'! Now I can use the cottage facilities when visiting my friends but enjoy my own cosy camper with a lovely field view.

"When I go down from there to Cardigan for an open mic night, the last thing I want is an hour's drive back afterwards. So when I go there, I park in an ordinary car park space, go to the open mic event and then just go to sleep in the camper.

y dweller Ruth likes to get away from it all in her camper

"When I visit friends, they don't have to clear the junk out of their spare room for me. Having a camper is nice compared to staying in a Travel Lodge or B&B."

Somewhere quiet to relax at work

Many people in southern England have a long commute to work, but not Ruth. She says, "I'm a live-in or pop-in carer. If I have time between appointments I can sit at my camper's table with a cup of tea or coffee. Being able to write or do a crossword in peace makes a huge difference. You could sit in a car, but it's not relaxing. If I'm going for a week for a live-in placement, I don't know what I might need. I have lots of things that just live in the campervan. When it comes to my two hours of free time in the afternoon, I often go out to relax in the van."

Folk festival fun

Ruth loves music and says, "The camper has a variety of different uses in my life, but it's a great enhancement to leisure. It's big enough for one woman and her guitar. I have always been a festival goer, but I'm getting a bit old and creaky to be doing it in a damp tent. Not only is staying in my campervan cosy, but I don't have to put up a blooming tent in the twilight when I'm sleepy, at the end of a long journey."

Steph and Chris bought their camper before starting a family, so Maddie has never known anything else

"Maddie is nearly two, and I'm expecting my second baby. We used the camper a lot before she was born and have been all around the UK, from Norfolk to North Devon and down to Pevensey on the South Coast.

"We've enjoyed all of the places we've visited and we have stayed a wide range of campsites! Our favourites have been the smaller, more independent ones with a hot shower for me and a fire pit for Chris.

"We first took Maddie away in 'Florence' the campervan when she was eight weeks old and it was so easy, she didn't know any different to being at home as long as she was warm and fed. We did have an incident with an explosive nappy which resulted in her having a bath in a bucket, but it was nothing we couldn't handle.

"We've enjoyed lots of trips and days out as a family of three - our last holiday being two weeks in the Vendée region of France last summer, which is the furthest we have been so far. We are going to have to make a few modifications if we are going to holiday as a family of four this year, but we are looking forward to many more adventures. We were only saying to each other recently, how lucky Maddie is to be growing up with a campervan in the family - there's nothing better!"

At 21 months, Maddie is already well-travelled

Having children might clip some young couples' wings - but not Chris & Steph

Cathie lives in a beautiful part of Devon, and since she has retired from teaching, she uses her CamperCar every day

She's had her camper for just a year, and says:

"I've always been a tent camper, but this is limited to summer. I wanted a longer camping season, so my CamperCar was the answer. I wanted something small and economical, because I use it for everything, but I go camping in it from March to October.

"I use it locally because I live in a beautiful part of the world. I'm not far from Woolacombe and Croyde, on the North Devon coast. In May, June and September, when you haven't got the holidaymakers, it's a good time to explore. I live in a beach area so when friends visit we take the CamperCar and use it as a changing room out of the wind, and make drinks in it."

Cathie's camper becomes a changing room at the beach

Chapter 16

Let your adventures begin

Bill & Elsa never miss a beautiful sunset, wherever they are

When it comes to campervanning, we have just one regret - that we didn't start earlier

Looking back, there are so many more things we could have done with our family - if only we'd bitten the bullet earlier.

We've made up for it. Over the last ten years we've been on countless trips in our campervan.

- We've explored all over the UK and Europe
- We've been wild camping
- We've stayed at amazing campsites in fantastic places
- We've discovered remote areas of the country we'd never otherwise have found
- We've met amazing people
- Our children have made new friends
- We've experienced other cultures and tried new foods

- We've helped ourselves escape from the stresses of everyday life
- We've enjoyed a lifestyle of freedom, spontaneity, and adventure

Most importantly of all, our campervans have brought us closer together as a family.

These experiences are far from unique. Many of our Sussex Campervans clients keep in close contact with us, sending emails and Facebook messages with photos or comments about their latest trips.

Manhattan campervan owner Georgie says:

"Just do it! It's the best investment we've made. We've had amazing holidays, and it doubles as our main motive for family outings."

Mobile Holidays

By Aprille

It has to be admitted that they all look much the same
Set out like a pack of cards all ready for a game.

Oblong metal boxes with windows and sliding doors
Fitted out with furniture and carpets on the floors.

Silently enduring winter's snow, sleet and rain
Waiting for good weather so they can spring to life again.

Then they're packed and filled and you might even see them grin
For the time has come at last to go and the holiday can begin.

The doors are all flung open and the windows open wide
As we're going on holiday and packing and busy inside.

Everyone is excited, there's chatting and laughter about.
"Don't forget the "Portaloo we must get it out."

Our 'home' is filled with practical things ready for a week.
We're off again on our travels as adventure is what we seek.

Maps and camera, a microwave to make mealtimes more easy.
Insect repellent, electric blanket and tablets in case I'm queasy!

Bags of food, a picnic lunch to have along the way.
'Glamping' is the buzzword, we're looking forward to our stay.

Almost ready to make a start, we'll leave early if we can.
Glowing with pride we'll enjoy the ride in our small red campervan.

You too could be part of this fun, flexible lifestyle.

We hope this book has given you an insight into 'Camper Van Life', as well as plenty of ideas to get you thinking about how you could use a campervan yourself.

If you'd like to find out more about owning your very own campervan conversion, we'd love to hear from you.

Daniel

& RebeKah